Attack on the Somme

Campaign Chronicles

Attack on the Somme

Haig's Offensive 1916

Martin Pegler

Campaign Chronicle
Series Editor:

Christopher Summerville

Pen & Sword
MILITARY

First published in Great Britain in 2005 by
Pen & Sword Military
An imprint of
Pen & Sword Books Ltd
47 Church Street
Barnsley
South Yorkshire
S70 2AS

ISBN 1 84415 397 5

A CIP catalogue record for this book is
available from the British Library

Printed and bound in England
By CPI UK

Pen & Sword Books Ltd incorporates the Imprints of Pen & Sword Aviation, Pen & Sword Maritime, Pen & Sword Military, Wharncliffe Local history, Pen & Sword Select, Pen & Sword Military Classics and Leo Cooper.

For a complete list of Pen & Sword titles please contact
PEN & SWORD BOOKS LIMITED
47 Church Street, Barnsley, South Yorkshire, S70 2AS, England
E-mail: enquiries@pen-and-sword.co.uk
Website: www.pen-and-sword.co.uk

Contents

List of Illustrations and Maps

Illustrations

Maps

Author's Note

A subject as vast and complex as the Battle of the Somme cannot be covered in depth in a single volume. The author has therefore tried to give a broad outline to the background of the war, as well as a brief comparative look at the armies and equipment involved. The length of the Somme campaign precludes an exhaustive study of every action involved, so the main objectives throughout the course of the campaign have been covered. If as a result, certain units or locations have been omitted, I can only offer my apologies. The quotations used are from veterans, most of whom the author was privileged to interview twenty or more years ago. To them, their families and all others who helped, I would like to offer my sincere thanks.

The photographs have been selected to try to provide some different images to the ones normally found in books on the Somme. They come from several sources, many from Richard Dunning's extensive collection, others from the archives of the Imperial War Museum, Tank Museum at Bovington and the Royal Armouries Museum, Leeds. I am most grateful to them all. I also extend my thanks to Editions de la Martinière, the publishers of Jacques Moreau's evocative photographic record of the war, *Nous Etions des Hommes*, for their kind permission to use some of his images. The maps are contemporary and are from the Official History of the War.

Finally, a special thank you to my wife Katie, who once again gave up any attempt at having a social life while I was writing another book, and who patiently corrected my many typographical mistakes. Any remaining errors are mine.

Epigraph

To ex-Private Clarence (Clarrie) Jarman, 7th Queens Royal West Surrey Regiment, my surrogate grandfather. Despite a lifetime of suffering as a result of fighting for King and Country, he never bore a grudge and typified the spirit of his generation. Also to Richard Dunning, owner and protector of the 'Lochnagar' crater at La Boisselle, whose deep appreciation of every aspect of the war and unselfish desire to share his knowledge with others to ensure we do not forget, are an object lesson to all of us.

Richard Dunning undertaking annual maintenance at Lochnagar crater, 2004.

Armistice Day 1986. Ex-Private Clarence Jarman, 7th Queens Regiment, aged eighty-eight.

Prologue

A German Machine-gunner at Serre, 1 July 1916

The following extract is taken from Experiences of Baden Soldiers at the Front, Volume 1: Machine-guns in the Iron Cross Regiment (8th Baden Infantry Regiment No. 169), by Otto Lais:

' "They're coming!" The sentries, who had to remain outside throughout the drumfire [the British artillery barrage], rise out of the shell holes. Dust and dirt lie a centimetre-thick on their faces and uniforms. Their cry of warnings rings piercingly in the narrow gaps that form the dugout entrance "Get out ... get out ... they're coming!" Now men rush to the surface and throw themselves into shell holes and craters; now they fling themselves in readiness at the crater's rim; now they rush forward under cover from the former second and third lines and place themselves in the first line of defence. There's a choking in every throat, a pressure which is released in a wild yell, in the battle-cry: "They're coming! They're coming!" Finally, the battle! The nightmare of this week-long drumfire is about to end; finally we can free ourselves of this week-long inner torment, no longer must we crouch in a flattened dugout like a mouse in a trap.

'The machine-gunners, who in quieter times were much mocked – and envied (excused from handling ammunition) – are popular now! One belt after another is raced through: 250 shots, 1,000 shots, 3,000 shots. "Bring up the spare gun barrels!" Shouts the gun commander. The gun barrel is changed. Carry on shooting – 5,000 shots – the barrel has to be changed again. The barrel is scorching hot, the coolant is boiling. The gunners' hands are nearly scorched, scalded. The coolant in the gun jacket boils, vaporized by the furious shooting. In the heat of battle, the steam hose comes away from the opening of the water can, into which the steam is meant to recondense. A tall jet of steam sprays upwards, a fine target for the enemy. It's lucky for us that the sun is shining in their eyes and that it's behind us.

'The enemy's getting closer. We keep up our continuous fire. The steam dies away, again the barrel needs changing. The coolant's nearly all vaporized. "Where is there water?" Shouts the gunlayer. There's soda water (iron rations from the dugout) down below. "There's none there, Corporal!" The iron rations were all used up in the week-long bombardment. Still the English attack: even though they already lie shot down in their hundreds in front of our lines, fresh waves continue to pour over from their jumping-off positions

'The skin of the gunners, of the gun commanders, hangs in shreds from their fingers, their hands are scalded! The left thumb is reduced to a swollen, shapeless piece of meat from continually pressing the safety catch. The hands grip the lightweight, thin gun handles, as if locked in a seizure. The platoon's other machine-gun jams. Gunner Schw– is shot in the head and falls over the belt that he feeds in. The belt is displaced, taking the cartridges at an angle into the feeder, where they become stuck. Another gunner takes over. The dead man is laid to one side. The gunlayer takes out the feeder, removes the cartridges and reloads.

'Shooting – nothing but shooting, barrel changing, handling ammunition and layout out the dead and wounded in the bottom of the trench: such is the harsh and furious pace of the morning of 1 July 1916. England's youth, Scotland's best regiments, bled to death in front of Serre. Our machine-gun, right by the Serre–Mailly road, commanded by the brave *Unteroffizier* [Corporal] Koch from Pforzheim, shoots through the last belt. It has driven twenty thousand shots into the English!

'After the initial confusion and panic caused by our unexpected resistance, after the horrific loss of life in their closely-packed attack formations, the English reform. For two hours and more, wave upon wave breaks against us. With incredible tenacity, they run towards our trenches. In an exemplary show of courage and self-sacrifice, they climb from the safety of their jumping-off position only to be felled, barely having reached our shot-up barbed wire. Twenty, thirty metres in front of our guns, the brave ones fall, the first and the last attack waves together.

'Those following take cover behind their dead, groaning and moaning comrades. Many hand, mortally wounded, whimpering, in the remains of the barbed wire and upon the hidden iron stakes of the barbed wire barricade. They make cover for themselves from the bodies of their dead comrades and many of us fall in the fire. We shoot the wire to shreds, into the belt of barbed wire that winds to the earth. The hail of bullets breaks up at the wire and strikes downwards as an unpredictable crossfire into the protective slope. Soon the enemy fire dies out here as well. The enemy's losses are inconceivable. In front of our division's sector, the English lie in rows by company and by battalion: mowed down, swept away ...'

Background

There are countless military campaigns whose glories have faded over time into distant memory and whose names would not now be remembered by any but a few dedicated historians. The Peninsular and Afghan wars, the Boer campaigns were all famous enough events in their day but are now lost in historical obscurity. However, some battles have remained in popular myth and memory as being of such importance that, while their broader details have been largely forgotten, their historical impact has remained with later generations. High on the list of such events are the battles of the Somme campaign, fought between July and November 1916. References to the Somme are still made and understood by the great-grandchildren of the soldiers who fought there nearly a century ago. It has now become a byword for brave but hopeless endeavour, enormous loss of life and the ultimate sacrifice of a generation of men. Ask almost any family about their own Great War history and it is almost certain you will be told of a relative who served and was wounded or died on the Somme.

How fair is this popular understanding of the battles that comprised the Somme offensive? Does it deserve to remain known in history simply for the terrible and unique level of casualties sustained on the first day of battle, or should the campaign be painted with a broader brush? All wars should be examined within the framework of their own historical context but sadly, once the survivors have faded away, each successive generation throws up a new layer of revisionists, apologists and accusers, who put their own opinions, values and theories on events. Was the outbreak of war in 1914 exactly as John Keegan stated, a 'tragic and unnecessary conflict' or was it simply an unstoppable event, a 'terrible inevitability' as Dr Gary Sheffield phrased it, that like a volcano, was simply awaiting the right moment to erupt? Certainly most historians are agreed the First World War came about as an inevitable consequence of British and German empirical desires. The build up to war had been a slow one, with Great Britain consolidating her position as a premier

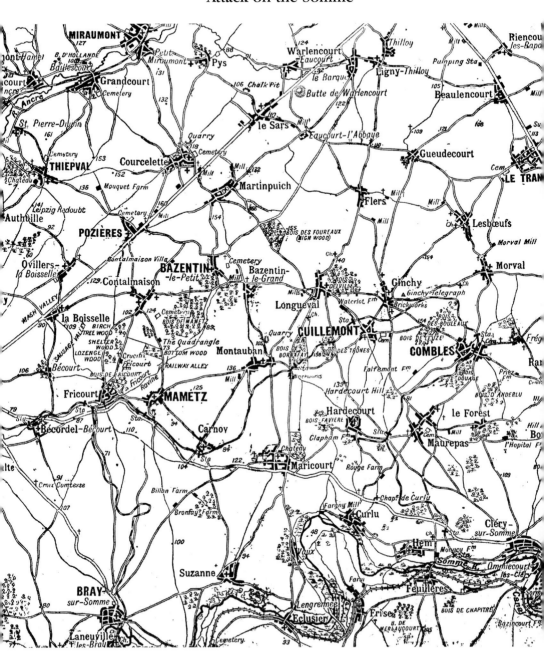

The position of the villages and woods of the Somme.

world colonial power, backed up by an immensely strong navy and small, but highly trained, professional army thinly spread around her colonial possessions. In opposition, and by no means the sole player in this game of military chess,

2

Background

was Germany. She had defeated the powerful Austrian Army in 1866 and went on to bring about the collapse of the old order in Europe by crushing France during the Franco-Prussian war of 1870–71. The unification of the thirty-nine German States in 1871 meant Germany had arguably become the most powerful European power by 1914. And not solely through its military dominance: for it was not Britain but Germany that — after the United States — was the biggest industrial power in the world. Germany had foreign aspirations too, and was a potent colonial power in its own right, particularly in East Africa. Other countries in Europe were also poised to enter centre stage in the political spotlight, not the least Russia, whose immense size made it a potentially formidable power, despite the poor equipment and training of its armies.

By 1910 there had been a number important changes in the demography and economies of the main European nations. Populations had expanded hugely in the previous two decades: 50 per cent in Russia, 43 per cent in Germany, 28 per cent in France, and 26 per cent in Britain. Industrial manufacture and inter-European trade was fundamental to the economies of all the European countries and advances in transport, specifically by railways and steam shipping, enabled raw materials, manufactured goods — and of course armies — to be more rapidly transported than at any previous time. Germany in particular had taken advantage of the importance of these improvements during the Franco-Prussian War, when it utilized its rail network to rush troops to the front line. However, that particular war was something of an exception, for diplomacy was the most powerful and widely used tool in defusing political crises during the first decade of the twentieth century. It was used most notably to smooth out the angst between Britain and Germany in Africa, and keep the factions from each other's throats in the Balkans. But the situation was exacerbated by Kaiser Wilhelm's dream of *Weltpolitik*, a dream that had disturbing undertones of later Nazism. This radically affected both France and Russia, who were justifiably wary of German expansionist dreams. Thus deep and simmering schisms had opened that seemed beyond the ken of the diplomats to close. And then there was the paranoia at the heart of the huge Austro-Hungarian Empire, whose Hapsburg rulers lived in constant fear of internal revolt. The empire encompassed five different religions, fourteen languages, and a complex history of political uprising and violence. Much of this originated in Serbia, a traditional hotbed of dissent and radical opposition. Vienna, meanwhile, was inextricably allied to Berlin. Italy, a country much influenced by Austria in the past, was deeply suspicious of the motives of the Central Powers, and her attempts to stay out of the conflict would be thwarted by Austrian attacks along her border.

Attack on the Somme

Summer 1914 and Kitchener Volunteers of the Lincolnshire Regiment pose with their Lee-Enfield rifles. At this time in the war most would remain in England for at least a year while they completed their training but many were destined to die on the Somme (Lincolnshire Museum).

Britain, meanwhile, was keeping a watchful eye on events but was unwilling to bestir itself, preferring to remain in what historians commonly refer to as 'splendid isolation'. Although wary of Germany, the British believed in the invincibility of their navy and were, in many respects, surprisingly tolerant of German expansionism. After all, it was not the Germans but the French who were our sworn enemies, and to whom many British regimental officers still raised their glasses after dinner with the words: 'Gentlemen, to our enemies, the French.' However, if there was one area the English did not regard as being negotiable, it was the neutrality of Belgium and its vital Channel coast. German moves against Belgium threatened Britain's security, her sea trade and her access to Europe. It was of little surprise, therefore, that when the German Army invaded Belgium in August 1914, the lion was forced to flex its claws and warfare was the inevitable consequence.

Background

Strategy

In 1905 Germany had drawn up a contingency plan for the invasion of France and Belgium called the Schlieffen Plan, after its originator. It relied on a surprise thrust through Belgium into France, knocking her out of the war before Russia could mobilize. Fortunately for the Allies, upon the outbreak of war the German Chief of Staff, von Moltke, decided against adhering to Schlieffen's model, redistributing the forces on his left wing, thus dooming the plan to failure. The race to the coast was lost by Germany and this was to have long-term consequences for the conduct of the rest of the war in France and Flanders. This was not the only problem the Germans faced though, for resistance was also much stiffer than the German High Command had planned for, and the area of conflict was expanding faster than Germany could contend with. Aside from France, the Belgian Army, such as was left, was still fighting in Flanders and both Russia and Italy were soon to be heavily engaged: Russia meeting the Germans in the East and tying up huge numbers of their troops; Italy clashing with the Austrians along her frontier and in the inhospitable Dolomites.

By 1915 the war had settled into a relatively static system of trench lines that ran from the Belgian coast to the Swiss border. Although the initial reaction from the Allies had been fragmented, it soon became clear that if all four powers could agree to launch an orchestrated assault on Germany and her allies, it was conceivable their combined weight would force Berlin to sue for peace. Germany could not afford to fight on two fronts indefinitely. By the autumn of 1915 there were already plans afoot for the British Expeditionary Force to launch a major assault in early 1916 in the troublesome Ypres Salient. This was to be followed by another offensive on the Somme in early spring. Inevitably there were problems, not least those of Russia: for after initial successes she had taken terrible losses on the Eastern Front and was unable to equip or train sufficient men to meet any serious commitment until at least the summer of 1916.

It was decided by the Alliance, therefore, that the best strategy to follow was an early offensive in Flanders, followed by a summer campaign on the Somme. But Germany pre-empted the Allies, launching a massive attack on the French forts in the Verdun region. Erich von Falkenhayn believed this offensive would 'bleed the French white'. The fact that the same might happen to his own army appears not to have concerned him. For the French soldiers and people, Verdun became a powerful symbol of defiance: 'On ne passeront pas' ('They shall not pass') became the French cry. Meanwhile, men and munitions were endlessly marched up the Bar-Le-Duc road, which quickly became known as the *le Voie Sacrée*, or the Sacred Way (although the *poilus* more accurately referred to Verdun as 'the mincing machine'). Naturally, such an unexpected strain on the French war effort was to have serious repercussions on any long-term strategic plans and the first casualty was the proposed Flanders offensive. This was a serious blow, as easy communication with the Channel ports would have materially assisted France's ability to sustain the battle. But the British were duty-bound to assist: though it is fair to say they were never happy with the options. Britain was now placed, militarily and politically, in an awkward position. She had to be seen to do her utmost to assist the French, yet by late 1915 the old Regular Army had all but vanished, and the brunt of the fighting would fall on a new Volunteer Army of 'Kitcheners Men', as yet an unknown quantity.

1914: The Casualties

Often dismissed as merely a series of small accidental battles, the first year of the war was to prove a costly series of encounters for all concerned. To put the level of fighting into context, casualties on the Western Front up to the end of 1914 alone were about 500,000 German, 349,000 French, and almost 74,000 British, most of whom were irreplaceable Regular Army soldiers. On the Eastern Front Germany lost a further 115,000 men and Russia some 362,000. While Germany had planned for a long war, in Britain the initial belief was that war would be short and sharp. This misconception faded quickly. Many British politicians and military commanders understood the magnitude of the task ahead. The Secretary of State, Lord Grey, had presciently remarked on 3 August 1914: 'The lamps are going out all over Europe. We shall not see them lit again in our lifetime.'

The Balance of Forces

Germany

The German Army was commanded by the Kaiser, Wilhelm II. By tradition a strong militarist, he had under him a number of experienced generals, of whom General von Moltke was Chief of the General Staff, although his failure to make the Schlieffen Plan work signalled his downfall, and he was replaced in September 1914 by Erich von Falkenhayn. The Germans had many experienced and intelligent officers, like von Kluck and von Below (First Army), von Bülow and von der Marwitz (Second Army), and Crown Prince Rupprecht of Bavaria (who personally commanded the Fifth Army). Many of the Regular officers were of the old Junkers class, who could trace their ancestry back to the Teutonic Knights of Medieval times. For them, leadership in any sphere of endeavour

A private in typical fighting order. Even without the addition of extra ammunition, grenades or trench impedimenta the average weight of his equipment was 60lb. The average height of an infantryman was 5 feet 8 inches, chest size 35 inches, and weight 135lb. Many men failed to reach even these modest standards due to poor diet (Royal Armouries).

was socially acceptable: but military service was considered appropriate for their class. The ordinary soldiers were also the product of a strongly militaristic society. Armed service was by conscription (not introduced in Britain until 1916), but such duty on behalf of their country was regarded by young Germans as both an honour and a moral obligation. The pre-war German Army comprised 800,00 men, but after mobilization in August 1914 this swelled to 4,500,000. Initially, most German soldiers believed they were fighting for the greater glory of the German Empire, but in the face of the punitive casualties of 1914, there is evidence that a year later men were already questioning the point of going to war. A number who discussed conditions with British troops during the Christmas truce of 1914 had expressed open doubt about the reason for the war and its eventual outcome.

Great Britain

The British were in many respects similar to their German counterparts in the quality of officers and men, their attitude, training and fighting spirit. The British Army was initially under the command of Sir John French, who was replaced in December 1915 by Sir Douglas Haig (who had until then been commander of the First Army). Haig has been much maligned over the years, yet he had been responsible for many necessary pre-war army reforms, and while no visionary, Haig was not the obdurate, blinkered general he is often made out to be. True, he was to an extent hidebound by his belief in the sanctity of the cavalry, whose use in an era of increasingly effective artillery and machine-guns was to be increasingly marginal, but it should be remembered that it was he who insisted the tank be put into military service as soon as possible. Under him were a host of experienced generals of the calibre of Rawlinson (Fourth Army), Gough (Fifth Army), and Allenby (Third Army). At regimental level, there was a strong body of professional officers, Sandhurst and Woolwich graduates, whose military lineage could often be traced back to Napoleonic times. At the outset of war many of these were also titled men, such as Major General the Hon. W. Lambton (4th Division) and the Hon. J.W. McCay (5th Australian Division). In common with their German counterparts, British officers on the Western Front suffered badly in the fierce fighting of 1914 and 1915, so by early 1916 a new breed of leaders was becoming evident, many of them ex-rankers promoted through ability. The same was happening in the ranks, as many time-serving Regular Army privates were promoted to senior NCO level to replace losses. This was no bad thing, for their experience provided the Volunteer Army of the Somme with a tough, battle-hardened backbone of men experienced in trench warfare. The tragedy was that so many would be dead or wounded by the end of the campaign. Small at the start of the war, with some 245,000 men in the Regular Army, the British Army soon comprised some 733,500 men, rising to 3,500,000 by 1916.

France

The pre-war French Army under Joffre's command was comparatively large with some 740,000 men under arms. By the time of the German invasion, mobilization had pushed this to about 3,780,000 men in uniform (slightly less than Germany). As with most other European countries, the generals were of the old school, steeped in tradition and the concept of *la Gloire*: dramatic cavalry charges, picturesque uniforms, and heroic battles. As a commander, Joffre was imperturbable, radiating an aura of calm confidence, and he was universally known by the *poilus* as 'Papa Joffre'. In reality, he had almost no tactical imagination and had difficulty grasping the overall strategic implications of the campaign he was commanding. Underneath him, among his many commanders, were three generals, Micheler, Fayolle, and Foch, who were to play an important part in the forthcoming battle. With their colourful, but impractical blue and red uniforms, old-fashioned small arms and equipment, it is arguable that France had the least modern army to take to the field in 1914. However, unlike the peacetime officers of Britain and Germany, there was not such a historical family tradition of military service, and many French officers were career soldiers who attended the French equivalent of Sandhurst College,

Background

Sir Douglas Haig and General Joffre in animated conversation with the Prime Minister, David Lloyd George (Royal Armouries).

the Saumur Military Academy. Many were men who had risen through the ranks by virtue of ability and this was an arguably better system than Britain's or Germany's, where social standing, wealth and tradition often determined the level and quality of the officer class.

The Start of the Conflict

Although the Great War is nowadays almost exclusively regarded as a land war, it should be remembered it was the Royal Navy that placed the greatest strain on Germany, for its blockade of German ports slowly began to strangle both the industry and social structure of Germany, and while it was not a quick process, it was an effective one. On land however, it was a different matter, for the BEF in France initially comprised of no more than 100,000 men. Although it was a tough and highly disciplined army, it was neither well led nor well versed in European military tactics, particularly on the scale that the coming war was to be fought. In addition, the *Entente Cordiale* was anything but cordial, as the British commanders were more or less forced to accede to the military demands of the French, who were themselves fighting desperately to keep the Germans at bay. The succession of bloody battles that swung to and fro across France and Belgium in 1914–15 was the death knell of the old Regular Army. The Marne, First Ypres, and the débâcle of Loos took their toll on an army that simply could not withstand the constant punishment inflicted on it by an enemy superior in both artillery and manpower. In 1914 the average casualty rate along the front was 14,500 men a day, and up to the end of 1915 the only successful engagement the British had fought was the Battle of Le Cateau. Meanwhile, England, historically untouchable across the protective waters of the Channel, had been bombarded from the sea by German battleships and bombed from the air by Zeppelins. In France, the first use of gas in April 1915 had caught the British, Canadians and Indian troops off-guard, and terrified soldiers retreated wholesale, having no means of protecting themselves. It was to be the start of war without rules.

Initially, the BEF was simply fighting to survive, having been thrust into the war with the primary aim of preventing the Germans reaching the Channel ports. But soon Britain was supporting, to its best abilities, French efforts to push the Germans from their soil, and in the wake of the dismissal of Sir John French, the appointment of General Sir Douglas Haig, as Commander-in-Chief was seen as a possible solution to what had clearly become a military stalemate. While Haig was expected to cooperate to the fullest extent with General Joffre, his appointment was also designed to enable the British Army, by then boosted with the arrival of tens of thousands of 'Kitchener Volunteers' to fight a war on its own terms. The major problem up to this point had been one of logistics: as Britain was obliged to fight on a scale never before experienced. Small-arms, uniforms, equipment, artillery, ships, aircraft and ammunition all had to be manufactured by what was essentially a peace-time industry, and such a massive undertaking took time to organize. In early 1915, British artillery units at the front were limited to three shells a day and the shell shortage was a major political scandal. It is a credit to the abilities of David Lloyd George, whose tenacity and understanding of the

Despite the images of mud and destruction, most veterans recalled the Somme as being a pleasant place to be when out of the line in summer. Here men are sleeping or playing cards besides their tents. The stacking of rifles was a practice that went back to Napoleonic times (R. Dunning collection).

plight of the British Army as senior Minister of War, meant that by the end of 1915 there were no shortages of anything, except perhaps sound military leadership. He was to become Prime Minister from December 1916.

The Weapons of War

The most important weapon on the battlefield, from the point of view of the soldiers, was the one that inflicted the most damage on either themselves or the enemy. Artillery technology had come a long way since the Boer War with light, quick-firing field guns that used a new system of hydraulic buffers to soak up recoil, as well as a range of larger, less mobile pieces. Howitzers could fire almost vertically, allowing shells to drop with tremendous destructive power, as the French found to their cost in their supposedly shellproof forts at Verdun. Larger guns could send their shells – weighing anything between 60 (27.2kg) and 1,400 pounds (635kg) – several miles quickly and accurately. By 1915 a new breed of naval gun, mounted on railway wagons, began to appear, with a destructive power beyond the comprehension of the average infantryman. The 12-inch railway gun, with its range of almost 33,000 yards (30,000m), fired a shell with a charge of 200 lb (90kg) of high explosive. This created an impact crater 30 feet (9.1m) wide and 20 feet (6m) deep: thus one projectile could wipe out an entire company of infantry. High explosive, shrapnel and gas shells were all in common use by the second year of the war, and artillery was responsible for more casualties than any other single weapon of war: some 58 per cent of the total. The technology was not only confined to the guns, for new forms of fuze began to appear, fitted to the shells themselves. Time activated shrapnel, impact, graze and delay fuzes all enabled the artillery to become more specialist, with artillerymen able to select different combinations of fuze- and shell-type depending on the target.

The Artillery

Artillery was rightly regarded as king of the battlefield. Guns varied in size from the relatively small British 13-pounder, with its 3-inch shell to the more common British 18-pounder, German 7.7cm and the famous French '75' quick-firer, which had a range of about 6,000 yards (5.4km). Short-barrelled howitzers could drop shells almost vertically onto their targets and the huge railway guns of 16- or 18-inch calibre could send shells over 20 miles (32km). The Germans bombarded Paris with a monstrous railway gun, whose shell rose to an altitude of 24 miles (38.6km) into the stratosphere and travelled almost 65 miles (104.6km) distance to its target. Only the machine-gun came close to artillery in its ability to inflict casualties.

The machine-gun had a troubled beginning, for the original heavy, slow firing and unreliable multi-barrelled weapons that were developed in the mid-nineteenth century had little practical application on the battlefield. The invention of the modern gun was due primarily to the mechanical genius of an expatriate American engineer, Hiram Maxim, who had taken up residence in

Background

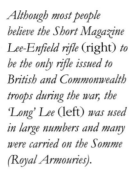

Although most people believe the Short Magazine Lee-Enfield rifle (right) *to be the only rifle issued to British and Commonwealth troops during the war, the 'Long' Lee* (left) *was used in large numbers and many were carried on the Somme (Royal Armouries).*

Britain in the 1880s. His constant attempts to harness the largely wasted energy generated by the cartridges led to the development of the Maxim gun, which reached its perfected form around 1908. From the outset these recoil-operated, belt-fed, water-cooled guns proved incredibly reliable and were adopted by many European countries, although most crucially by Germany, Russia and Great Britain, albeit in slightly differing forms. Capable of firing at up to 500 rounds a minute, they were, as one contemporary commentator noted, turning warfare into 'automated death'. France had adopted a simpler but equally effective Hotchkiss gun and Austria the *Schwartzlose*. In the countless infantry assaults that characterized the course of the war, and the Somme battles in particular, it was the machine-gun that was to tear the heart out of attacking forces, decimating entire battalions in the space of a few minutes, its metallic chatter equally loathed and feared by all sides.

The old single-shot black powder rifles had quickly fallen into disuse when in 1886 the French invented a self-contained metallic cartridge containing a new smokeless powder called nitro-cellulose. It gave a range and accuracy to service rifles that had hitherto been a dream, and by the turn of the century, virtually every army in Europe had adopted similar weapons. These fired high velocity bullets of comparatively small calibre, about 8mm/.30 inch and used a rotating bolt to load and chamber a cartridge. Most were magazine-fed weapons, and could hold between three and ten rounds depending on the type of rifle. Maximum range was well in

13

Attack on the Somme

The architects of the Somme defence: General Hindenberg, Kaiser Wilhelm II and General Ludendorff. By the end of the war Ludendorff almost had sole control of the German Army (Bundesarchiv).

excess of 1,000 yards (914.4m) and they could be loaded and fired as fast a soldier could work the bolt, the British Army priding itself on its ability to fire fifteen aimed rounds a minute. All rifles could be fitted with a sword or socket bayonet for close combat, although it made them unwieldy in trench fighting. Amazingly, in 1914 most British officers were still armed with swords, which aside from being useless on the modern battlefield, made them a ready target for snipers. Officers also routinely carried pistols, the British and French favouring revolvers, while Germans invariably carried semi-automatics. British officers could carry any make of pistol provided it chambered the standard .455 inch cartridge. German officers and NCOs were issued with 9mm Lugers but many chose to carry privately purchased semi-automatic pistols such as the Mauser C96 'Broomhandle'. In the early war period pistols were of little use, as their range was so limited, but as trench warfare became the norm, they were soon an indispensable item for close-quarter fighting. As were hand-grenades. Initially of the simplest type, being little more than cast iron cylinders packed with explosive with a slow-burning fuse, by 1914 Germany had introduced the relatively sophisticated 'defensive' stick grenade, actuated by a pull-cord and containing a hefty explosive charge. Britain, France and Italy all developed 'offensive' grenades, relying not on explosive content, but fragmentation to kill or disable, and most used a time-fuse, although impact detonated grenades were not uncommon. The British 'Mills bomb' was to become an almost universal symbol of trench fighting, and during the war some 60 million were manufactured.

Background

Infantry Weapons

By 1916 machine-guns were using more powerful ammunition than rifles and the Vickers-Maxim could deliver harassing fire at a range of 3,500 yards (3.2km). The introduction of the Lewis light machine-gun in 1915 gave British troops a considerable edge in mobile firepower, being capable of firing at a rate of 550 rounds a minute. The extreme range of a rifle bullet was about 2,500 yards (2.2km) but the average combat distance was under one 150 yards. At 200 yards (182.8m) a rifle bullet could penetrate 9 inches (228mm) of bricks, 18 inches (457mm) of sandbags or 4 feet 6 inches (1.37m) of loosely packed earth.

The Royal Flying Corps

While preparations for the battle largely involved land forces, the RFC was to provide vital assistance for the army. The advances made in aircraft technology by 1916 had surpassed anything that could have been predicted in 1914. This is even more astonishing when one realizes there was no air force at all in existence in Britain before 1912. Since the outbreak of war, the types of aircraft and the uses to which they were put had changed beyond all recognition. The flimsy, primitive aeroplanes of the early war period, such as the Maurice Farman and BE2c had been rapidly replaced by sturdier aircraft with specialist roles: fighters such as the Sopwiths, observation and bomber aircraft like the RE8, and the priceless RFC-crewed observation balloons, whose podgy white forms hung in a curtain along the front, watching every move the Germans made. Nor should Haig's openness to new technology be undervalued, for he saw uses for the air force that were beyond the understanding of the majority of army commanders. Like Haig, Major General Hugh Trenchard, commander of the RFC believed in the value of staying on the offensive and wearing down the enemy. As plans for the Somme were being laid, Trenchard was given the most powerful air force that Britain had ever possessed, with some twenty-seven squadrons that comprised almost 490 aircraft of various types. Their tasks were threefold. Target spotting, to detect enemy artillery and troop formations, provision of harassing attacks by bombing or strafing of German positions, and protection of the British front from enemy air observation, by keeping away German aircraft and destroying their observation balloons. This they did with considerable effectiveness, although at a cost, for by the end of the Somme campaign the RFC had lost almost twice its strength in aircraft and about 580 pilots. The Germans had long been ahead of everyone else in the technological air race, producing powerful engines, well-designed fighters and reconnaissance aircraft, and developing the mechanism for enabling a machine-gun to be fired through a rotating propeller. It would be wrong to suggest the RFC had mastery of the skies at any time during the Somme campaign, but they did manage – against all odds – to

The Germans had recognized the potential of the machine-gun long before the British, and machine-gun companies were an integral part of every German regiment. Here a crew pose with their sledge-mounted Maxim 08. The crew normally consisted of six men, all of whom were trained machine-gunners. The youth of some of them is obvious (Author's collection).

ensure the Germans were unable to use their aircraft to their full advantage, and this materially assisted the Allies in their conduct of the campaign.

The Plan of Attack

To ensure there were sufficient men available for the campaign, the British High Command had little option but to send the newly raised Territorial Divisions to France. Initially, Haig was not in favour of this, knowing them to be untested in

battle, and he was doubtful their training or discipline was sufficient to enable them to meet the tough German Army on equal terms. Still, he believed the new plan was capable of achieving what the battles of 1915 had not.

There was little doubt that among the volunteers of 1914 and early 1915, morale was incredibly high. They had seen the old army melt away and many had lost friends and relatives in the fighting. They wanted, as eighteen-year-old volunteer Clarence Jarman put it, 'Just to have a crack at the Huns.' He was soon to have his chance, with thousands of others. In early 1916, while the training regiments based in England marched, countermarched, and incessantly dug trenches across any piece of available ground, a new plan was being hatched. French losses, particularly at Verdun were becoming almost unsupportable, and Joffre believed a diversionary attack was urgently needed. Haig was honour-bound to accede to this but knew that even in the event of a successful outcome of a battle somewhere on the Somme, Britain and her allies still could not hope to end the war in 1916. It might, however, force the German Army to relocate large numbers of men from the beleaguered French sector, and at the same time inflict heavy losses on them, while enabling the British Army to push forward to open ground, where they would be in a favourable position to defeat the Germans, hopefully in 1917. To achieve this, the main weight of the attack was to be borne by General Sir Henry Rawlinson's Fourth Army, along a frontage on the Somme of roughly 13 miles (20.9km), running south and slightly east from the village of Hebertune, at the northernmost edge of the front, down to the French lines at Maricourt, just to  the north of the River Somme. North of Hebertune, the Third Army, under General Sir Edmund Allenby, would be holding the line, and a Reserve Army, commanded by General Sir H. Gough, was to be kept in the wings to capitalize on any breakthrough. The French Sixth Army held the ground south of the river.

The plan was to simultaneously assault the first line of German trenches that ran from Serre to Maricourt, mostly on the vital high ground, rolling it back some 2,000 yards (1.8km) and then occupying it. On the northern flank, the Third Army was to attack Gommecourt and its salient, and the Fourth Army was to take Montauban, Contalmaison, Pozières, Miramont and Serre. Initial success here was crucial in allowing the Fourth Army to be in a position to attack the weak German third lines and break through into open country without being

Artillery bombardment was a vital part of the preparations for the Somme offensive, and guns of every calibre were employed. Here a crew of Royal Artillerymen, stripped to the waist, lay a 9.2-inch howitzer. The hydraulic buffers above the barrel help to soak up the recoil (R. Dunning).

enfiladed by German gunfire. One of the major drawbacks of the plan was that, from Haig downwards, none of the army commanders were experienced in handling the numbers of troops that would be under them. In the case of the Fourth Army, this would be some twenty-five divisions. Pre-war, no one had ever remotely considered the possibility of Britain fielding an army the size of the one now gathering in France. It was truly a case of the blind leading the blind. Yet Haig had little option, for in the likelihood of the French giving way at Verdun, the front would be left wide open, and the chances of preventing a wholesale German advance virtually non-existent. Yet to put such a strategy into action in a relatively short period of time required detailed planning: the movement of tens of thousands of men, as well as shells, rations, artillery and ammunition limbers, medical supplies, and all of paraphernalia of modern war. Of the 660,000 men in the BEF in early 1916, some 400,00 were to be involved in the offensive. It is almost impossible to conceive the logistical problems involved in such a task. The Royal Artillery's demands alone were colossal: 2.6 million rounds of 18-pounder ammunition was to be supplied, as well as 100,000 rounds of 6-inch howitzer, and these represented only two calibres of artillery, there were also 60-pounders, 4.5-inch and 9.2-inch and 15-inch howitzer, as well as railway guns. The Fourth Army alone required some 1,500 guns of assorted calibres to be fed with ammunition, which required one million shells of all calibres *a week*. A crucial task for the Royal Artillery was in planning a bombardment that would knock out German batteries, destroy the deep dugouts along the front line, and most crucially for the attacking troops, break up the impenetrable belts of wire that ran in front of the German trenches along the entire front. The opening barrage began on the 24 June and was to continue up to 'Z' day, 29 June. The offensive was planned to start at dawn the following morning.

The Royal Artillery were not fighting a one-sided war, however, and suffered heavily from retaliatory fire during their pre-attack bombardment. Gunner C. Burrows of the 104th Battery, Royal Field Artillery wrote in his diary on 25th June: 'One gunner blown to pieces, one sergeant and gunner wounded, one gun pit wrecked by a direct hit . . .' If there were any weakness in the artillery plans, it was an underestimation of the strength of the German dugouts, formidable concrete-lined structures often 30 feet (9.1m) underground, as well as the mistaken belief that shrapnel shells were capable of cutting barbed wire. Such simple mistakes were to cost many lives. In terms of manpower, there were eleven army corps to be engaged, including one Canadian and one ANZAC, comprising some fifty-three divisions, as well as the newly formed Heavy Branch, Machine-gun Corps (Tanks). These divisions were gradually gathering on the Somme after having undertaken some physically punishing night marches to enable them to reach their destinations without being spotted by enemy observers. In three nights some regiments marched nearly 50 miles (80.4km), leaving the soldiers utterly exhausted. Others, like the 7th Queens Royal West Surrey Regiment, were already in the lines near La Boisselle and had been for some weeks. Private Jarman recalled being 'keen to get to the Germans because we couldn't get any rest due to the cramped conditions and constant German shellfire.' Others came from further afield, the 29th Division arriving from the débâcle of Gallipoli and entering the trenches opposite Beaumont Hamel,

Background

The Infantryman

The arms and equipment carried by the average infantryman varied depending on his unit and circumstances, but aside from uniform, helmet, webbing or leather equipment, ammunition pouches, bayonet, rifle, pack, water bottle and rations, he could also be carrying extra ammunition, slung pouches of hand-grenades, a shovel or even coils of wire for field telephones. The total weight was anything from 60–80 lb (27–36kg), which is about the same as that of a Medieval suit of armour. Instructions for the men to walk, not run when attacking seem somewhat superfluous.

---

where a large placard stood in the German lines, welcoming them to the front! As the plan was to start the attack at dawn on the 30 June, the soldiers did their best to get some rest under the constant thunder of thousands of guns. As the hour of attack grew inexorably closer, aside from a few Regular battalions, the newly raised British Territorial regiments were assembling on, or close behind, the front line. Almost all of them were county regiments, from Dorset, Surrey, Berkshire, the Midlands, Yorkshire, Wales, Durham, Lowland and Highland Scotland. From all over the country, groups of workmates, friends, country- and city-dwellers had enlisted, trained and been transported to France together. Many were the so-called Pals Battalions, comprising men from the same streets, factories or cities. Aside from bursting enthusiasm they all shared one thing, they were volunteers, not one of them was a conscript.

For the Germans, the bombardment was a frightening experience as the British artillery ceaselessly pounded their lines, preventing relief or resupply. Private F. Eversmann of the 143rd Infantry Regiment endured days of shelling in his dugout on the front line at Thiepval:

'25th June 7 o'clock: The barrage has now lasted thirty-six hours. How long will it go on ?

'25th June, 10 o'clock: Veritable *Trommelfeuer* (drumfire). In twelve hours shelling they estimate 60,000 shells have fallen . . . when will they attack ? Tomorrow or the day after? Who knows?

'27th June, 4am: There must be an end sometime to this horrible bombardment. . . .

'It is night. Shall I live till morning? Haven't we had enough of this frightful horror? Five days and five nights now this hell's concert has lasted. How long is it going to last?'

Campaign Chronicle

Eversmann was never to know, for his diary was later found on his body. For the waiting British troops, the last few hours were the worst. Private Jarman, of the 7th Queens was waiting nervously, when word came through the attack was postponed: 'At the very last moment it was cancelled. The weather had turned awful and we were stuck in our trenches in torrential rain, with no cover.' Weather conditions now conspired to turn the trenches into streams and the heavy chalk soil into white putty. There was nothing for it but to sit it out. Men wrote last letters home, cleaned already spotless rifles, or prayed quietly. The inevitable platoon wags cracked jokes, at which some

The use of observation balloons by both sides was crucial in enabling observers to spot troop movements or the digging of fresh defences. Although vulnerable to fighter attack, they were invaluable and usually heavily protected by anti-aircraft guns. This is a British balloon being prepared for launching, watched by a crown of curious Tommies (R. Dunning).

1 July: The Attack on Gommecourt

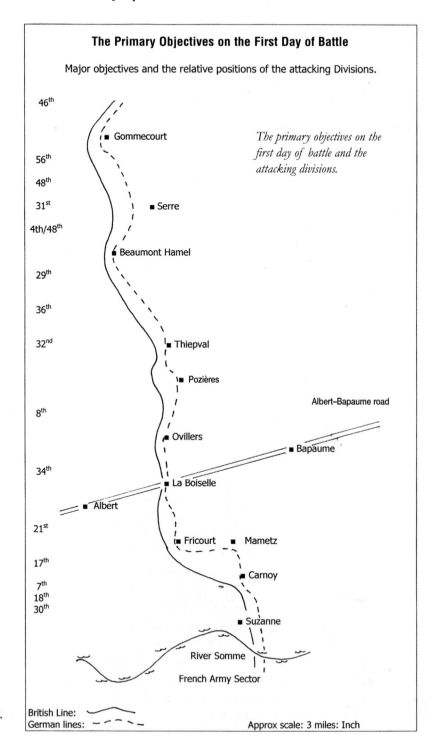

The Primary Objectives on the First Day of Battle

Major objectives and the relative positions of the attacking Divisions.

46th

56th

48th

31st

4th/48th

29th

36th

32nd

8th

34th

21st

17th

7th
18th
30th

■ Gommecourt

The primary objectives on the first day of battle and the attacking divisions.

■ Serre

Beaumont Hamel

■ Thiepval

■ Pozières

Albert–Bapaume road

■ Ovillers

■ Bapaume

■ La Boiselle

■ Albert

■ Fricourt   ■ Mametz

■ Carnoy

■ Suzanne

River Somme

French Army Sector

British Line:
German lines:

Approx scale: 3 miles: Inch

23

laughed and others muttered curses. At 7.30am on 1 July a sudden and eerie hush fell over the front as the British artillery ceased fire. Whistles blew and scaling ladders shook as men scrambled up them into No Man's Land. The battle had begun.

1 July: The Attack on Gommecourt

At the furthest northerly point of the attack, VII Corps of the Third Army, under General Allenby, which comprised the 56th (London) and 46th (North Midland) Divisions, was to attack the German lines from the north and south, using a pincer movement to capture Gommecourt, in the hope of flattening the awkward German salient that bulged into British lines. It would also create a diversion to draw German divisions northwards, away from the central thrust of the Somme attack. Having captured the village, the divisions would then link to form an extended line. But there was no doubt the Germans had a very clear idea of what was happening, with intelligence reports stating: 'The new British assault trenches . . . the frequent bombardment . . . the appearance of heavy trench mortars and the increasing artillery fire . . . left no doubt as to the intention of the enemy.'

For the battalions comprising the 46th Division, the task of capturing Gommecourt appeared a feasible objective. Along the front many battalion commanders had moved their men out of the front line into newly dug jumping-off trenches in No Man's Land, called Russian Saps, which had the twin-advantages of avoiding German shelling, while placing the attackers closer to their objectives. The artillery had been instructed to bombard the German lines until Zero Hour, when they would raise their sights to begin a 'creeping barrage', behind which the men could advance in relative safety. The soldiers had been ordered to fix bayonets and to advance in line abreast, with rifles at the port, as it was felt unlikely they would meet heavy return fire. Most commanders expected their men would easily advance over the shattered German front line, perhaps pausing here and there to round up a few dazed prisoners. As whistles blew at 7.25am, the men rose from their trenches into an unexpected storm of enemy shell and machine-gunfire. It appeared the diversionary plan to draw the Germans' attention was working all too well. From the outset the attack went badly, with enemy fire wreaking havoc among the advancing troops. The British smokescreen was drifting back into the faces of the advancing troops, confusing officers and men. As the smoke cleared, troops reached the German wire to find it horribly intact. Despite heavy enfilade machine-gunfire, two battalions of the Sherwood Foresters managed

1 July: The Attack on Gommecourt

to break into the front line, but they became trapped by Germans emerging from dugouts all around them. The maze of trenches and saps the attacking battalions had occupied now became a killing ground for the defenders, who could attack from front, rear or flank. Parties of British soldiers fought valiant holding actions and it was mostly point-blank fighting with grenades, bayonets and revolvers: the plaintive message being constantly flashed back by signal lamp 'SOS BOMBS SOS BOMBS.' Supply parties were sent into the maelstrom to deliver cases of Mills bombs and .303 inch ammunition, but few made it there and none made it back. By afternoon, reserve troops had been sent forward, but most became casualties as a result of heavy fire from machine-guns and artillery. Eventually, the fire from the beleaguered troops began to die down, and it became clear to the observers in the front-line trenches the Germans must have overwhelmed them. Early in the evening, a single Lewis gun could still be heard chattering, but eventually that too fell silent. It was a credit to the 46th Divisional commander, Major General Hon. E.J. Montague Stuart-Wortley, that he refused to commit more men to the assault, realizing it was fruitless. He was replaced on 5 July.

The amount of ammunition required to feed the artillery was prodigious. This photographs shows a small part of a British dump of 8-inch howitzer shells on the Somme in summer 1916. A hit from an enemy shell would prove catastrophic (Royal Armouries).

Meanwhile, the two brigades of the 56th (London) Division attacked simultaneously and plodded resolutely forwards, fortunately finding the wire shredded, with the German lines pulverized into mounds of white chalk and bodies. But the further they went, the heavier became the resistance. German machine-gunners in the reserve lines pulled their Maxims up the steep steps and slapped ammunition belts into them. It took less than a minute to set up a gun and have it firing, and they were desperate to get their own back on an enemy who had pounded them so mercilessly for so many days. In particular, a strongpoint called Nameless Farm was heavily defended, and with the aid of some field guns, the German infantrymen fought the battalions of the 56th Division to a standstill. Captain A.L. Agius MC, of the 1/3rd City of London Regiment, had miraculously survived the attack: 'We got orders to turn and make our way back to the village. One of my Subalterns was newly out. Such a nice chap He . . . just disappeared in an explosion. I heard a shell coming. Just imagine hearing a single shell in the middle of all this din! It burst just above my head. The sergeant was blown one way and I was blown the other. He was killed. I don't know how I got back. It was murder.'

The German artilleryfire increased to a pitiless crescendo, preventing the deployment of reinforcements, and the British occupying the trenches — although partly protected from the barrage — had to contend with ferocious attacks by German troops. The wounded tried to return to the British lines, but few could survive the shells or machine-gunfire. By 4pm the second line trench had been re-taken by the Germans. At nightfall, less than eighty officers and men returned, leaving some 1,300 dead behind them. There was little question the whole attack had been a dismal failure, and this was to have repercussions along the whole front, leaving the northernmost sector wide open and permitting the Germans to render crucial assistance to the centre and south of the attack area. The VII Corps had lost over 6,700 men for no tactical gain at all.

1 July: The Attack on Serre

Three miles (4.8km) south of Gommecourt, at the southernmost edge of the VII Corps flank, VIII Corps, under Major General R. Wanless O'Gowan, contained the 4th, 29th and 31st Divisions. In particular, the 31st was full of pride and promise, for it contained many of the Pals Battalions, raised in the industrial heartland of the north, among them The East Yorks and West Yorks Regiments, Durham Light Infantry, and Yorks and Lancs Regiment. The plan was for the village of Serre to be overrun, then a right turn would be executed

The immense amount of supplies required had to be carried up to the front by mules or wagons. This became impossible when the weather deteriorated and the roads became quagmires. In the later stages of the campaign, even mules were unable to reach the trenches. Here they are carrying loads of petrol cans, probably containing water (R. Dunning).

to form a strongpoint to defend the rest of the line against a possible German counter-attack on the Fourth Army flank. Men who had known each other from childhood wished each other good luck, shook hands, then slipped through their own wire and lay down in No Man's Land to await Zero Hour. As they rose into the clear sunshine the Maxims began their rhythmic 'tac-tac-tac' and few of the troops advanced more than 100 yards (91.4m) before falling to the hail of bullets. One of those shooting at them was Musketeer Karl Benk, 169th (8th Baden) Regiment: 'We were very surprised to see them walking, we had never seen that before. I could see them everywhere, there were hundreds. When we started firing, we just had to load and reload. They went down in their hundreds. You didn't have to aim, we just fired into them. If only they had run they would have overwhelmed us.' Most of those Pals who had enlisted such a short time before with such patriotic fervour had either died or been wounded. Many lay hidden in shell holes, praying they would be spared to crawl back to their trenches when dusk fell. Miraculously, some units did manage to reach their objective: a few of the 12th York & Lancs and 11th East Lancs disappearing into the edge of the village, never to be seen again. Some men of the 18th Durham Light Infantry even advanced as far as a small wood, Pendant

Copse, over a mile from the British front line. They too disappeared, their remains being found when the village was finally taken in November. As with the Gommecourt attack, the assault had petered out by mid-afternoon and no further attempt was made to renew it. The division lost 3,600 men in a matter of hours and no ground was taken.

1 July: The Attack on Beaumont Hamel

Slightly south of Serre, the other elements of VIII Corps had managed to capture their objective. Unusually, there were two divisions, the 4th and 29th, that still comprised Regular Army battalions, and their tough professionalism enabled them to reach the heavily defended Heidenkopf or Quadrilateral Redoubt. Their assault was assisted, to some extent, when a huge mine containing 40,000 pounds of Ammonal was blown under the German Hawthorn Redoubt at 7.20am, collapsing dugouts and entombing hundreds of men. The timing of the mine had been a matter of some dispute, for General Hunter-Weston wanted it blown four hours before the attack, so it could be occupied before the Germans knew what had happened. But GHQ had issued orders that all mines were to be fired no earlier than eight minutes before Zero. Hawthorn was in fact blown ten minutes in advance, but this unfortunately coincided with an error in orders that instructed the artillery to lift their barrage at the same time, so for ten vital minutes, there was no artillery cover for the advancing troops. The detonation of the mine acted as a signal to the waiting Germans, who quickly swarmed out of their dugouts, with the result that as platoons of the 2nd Royal Fusiliers rushed forward, they found the smoking crater already occupied. The 1st Rifle Brigade and 1st East Lancs had found the German wire destroyed, and despite heavy fire, entered the Quadrilateral Redoubt, to be reinforced with elements from the Royal Warwickshire and Somerset Light Infantry. But they were unable to consolidate their gains and were eventually driven out with heavy casualties (4,700 men) next day.

Meanwhile, the rest of the neighbouring 29th Division had formed up opposite Beaumont Hamel and their advance was to be almost a carbon copy of the events at Serre: for as the men rose from their trenches the Germans of the 119th (1st Württemberg) Regiment could not believe their luck at the targets that presented themselves. Many Germans stood *on top* of their parapets to allow themselves better aim. With no artillery support the attack was doomed and by 9am men were falling back. Tragically, an incorrect report reached the divisional HQ stating Beaumont Hamel had been taken and at 9.30am the 1st Newfoundland Regiment was ordered forward as support. As they moved in an extended line towards the enemy they fell in their hundreds to the concentrated fire. One unnamed German machine-gunner later said the slaughter was so great that afterwards some of his comrades wept as they sat exhausted on their fire-step. Over 700 men of the Newfoundlands became casualties, 91 per cent of the total, and by 11am the attack was abandoned. Along the VIII Corps front no gains had been held and the corps had the dubious distinction of losing more men on the day than any other, some 14,000 in all.

1 July: The Attack on Thiepval

Despite the strenuous efforts made by the officers and men of the 29th Division, they had made little or no headway against the German defences on the western area of Allenby's Third Army. The failure to take and hold any worthwhile objectives meant that along the rest of the Somme front, divisions would be pushing forward with their flanks wide open, and this was particularly true of the 36th (Ulster) Division, which comprised the Irish Rifle and Fusilier battalions. The problem was exacerbated by the geographical location of their objective, the village of Thiepval, which lay on a spur at the western end of the meandering Pozières Ridge. Although the intense British bombardment had reduced the village to brick dust, in the cellars and dugouts tunnelled beneath the ruined houses, German soldiers waited for the barrage to lift: deafened, uncomfortable, but safe enough from all but the largest shells. The Germans' big advantage, which was to cost the attacking Irishmen so dearly, was that from the heights they could enfilade the British line of advance for as far as the eye could see.

The plan was for the corps to capture Thiepval and its plateau, with the 36th Division on the left moving along the Ancre Valley to take St Pierre Divion, and the 32nd Division, a mixed New Army unit, on the right. They had the unenviable task of taking the Thiepval spur, hopefully capturing the village and the heavily fortified Leipzig Redoubt. The 32nd Division had been sensibly deployed in advance of their trenches and the 17th Highland Light Infantry were almost within hand-grenade distance of the German lines when Zero Hour arrived. They rushed the gaps in the wire and captured part of the Leipzig Redoubt, sending prisoners back. This was risky for the prisoners, as heavy German machine-gunfire was raking the ground. One soldier wrote of seeing: 'A group of Germans with their hands raised, fall like corn as they were caught by a machine-gun firing from Thiepval.' These guns were to reap terrible destruction on the attacking formations, for as the advancing troops moved across the German trenches into open ground, they became easy targets for the Maxims situated in the Schwaben Redoubt: a massively fortified position that dominated the ground from behind Thiepval village. Men fell like flies, with nowhere to hide from the merciless fire of the guns, and when the 11th Border Regiment left their cover in nearby Authuille Wood, they sustained 50 per cent casualties within yards. Lance Corporal F. Allan recalled that: 'The colonel was fidgeting . . . and eventually decided to lead them on himself but as soon as he left the trench he was shot through the head and killed. Then the adjutant was severely wounded as he leaned over the colonel's body. The second in command had already been wounded.' The battalion was effectively leaderless and the men were forced to retreat to the Leipzig Redoubt, which they held despite strenuous German efforts to evict them.

As the barrage lifted at Zero Hour, the Ulstermen on the left were less than 100 yards (91.4m) from the German lines, having also crept forward under cover of their own shellfire. At 7.30am they rose as their buglers sounded 'advance'. They were close enough to catch the Germans as they emerged from their dugouts and initially they did well, taking the first and second lines and heading for the Schwaben Redoubt, which they assaulted in fine style, capturing over 400 prisoners. They continued despite heavy casualties until they reached the switch line of Mouquet Farm, and by 9am reserve troops comprising 9th, 10th and 11th Royal Inniskilling Fusiliers and the 11th Royal Irish Rifles attempted to advance across No Man's Land, but suffered the consequences courtesy of the mistimed British barrage, which caught them in the open. The attack faltered and this enabled the machine-guns to pour more fire into the Ulstermen from the rear left flank. They were pinned down and had little alternative but to stay put. For some, their first experience of battle was to leave scars that would never fade. Private R. Irwin, 9th Royal Enniskillen Volunteers recalled sixty years later: 'I was firing on some Germans when there was a loud explosion near me and part of the torso of a man clothed in a khaki jacket landed just in front of my Lewis gun.' Headquarters had little idea of the situation and even ordered the 49th Division (West Riding) Territorials forward to reinforce the flagging attack, but it was hopeless. The trenches were choked with wounded, there were exhausted soldiers slumped everywhere, with fresh troops vainly attempting to push through and keep in contact with their guides. As the day progressed increasing German counter-attacks forced the men back from the redoubts and by night most were back where they had started. German reports talk of 'a wall of British dead piled up on the front'. Of the 9,000 casualties sustained by X Corps over half were the brave Ulstermen.

1 July: The Attacks on Ovillers and La Boisselle

South of Authille Wood and the ill-fated Thiepval attack, was Lieutenant General Sir E.W. Pulteney's III Corps, facing the villages of Ovillers and La Boisselle, with Fricourt village on his extreme southern flank. These villages were situated on two geographical spurs, in front of which ran the main Albert–Bapaume road. The two valleys that ran between these spurs were christened, with typical British humour, 'Sausage' and 'Mash' Valleys. Strongpoints had been built by the Germans on the high ground and all were protected the protruding bulk of the Thiepval spur to the north. It was perfect for defence and incredibly difficult to attack. Nevertheless, it was the centre for the assault of III Corps' 34th (New Army) Division and the 8th (Regular) Division. It was undoubtedly a tough nut to crack and the British had for some

In an effort to protect the roads from observation, the British made use of camouflage netting, which was strung for hundreds of yards along many of the busier routes. Although it prevented direct observation, most German artillery fired by map reference, and the covering provided little material benefit. Known danger points were invariably taken at a run or gallop (Author's collection).

months been tunnelling under the German lines at La Boisselle. Two mines, named New Crater (later known as 'Lochnagar') and Y Sap had been finished and filled with explosive. The men would be advancing with a rolling barrage in front of them scheduled to move at precisely 2 miles (3.2km) in one hour forty-seven minutes. At 7.28am on 1 July both mines were detonated, mostly under the trenches occupied by the 110th (2nd Baden) Infantry. It was observed by cameraman Geoffrey Malins: 'The ground where I stood gave a mighty convulsion. It rocked and swayed. Then (looking) for all the world like a giant sponge, the earth rose high in the air . . . higher and higher it rose and with a horrible grinding roar the earth settle back upon itself, leaving in its place a mountain of smoke.' Hundreds of Germans were killed instantly in their dugouts, unknown numbers of others were buried. Two minutes later, to the shrill of whistles, the twelve battalions of the Division left their trenches and advanced. Comprised of Northumberland Fusiliers, with battalions of the Royal Scots, Lincolnshire and Suffolks, they were typical New Army men, keen to prove their mettle, but led by inexperienced officers and NCOs. They advanced towards the German defences in open file, in three neat, serried ranks 400 yards (365.7m) apart, across defences that had barely suffered from the British barrage, the deep dugouts impervious to the rain of shells. Despite the damage inflicted by the mines, the German machine-gunners and riflemen swarmed from their battered trenches and occupied the lip of the smoking craters. They were met by the sight of lines of advancing men, bayonets glittering in the early sunlight. It took about ten minutes for 80 per cent of these attacking British soldiers to be killed or wounded. So quickly were they mown down, the German machine-gunners didn't even have time to change the red-hot barrels of their guns. Few survived the murderous short-range hail of bullets. Private L. Dodd, 4th Tyneside Scottish had marched steadily forward and reached the front-line German trenches. He looked around and was surprised to see: 'only three of our company . . . there was my lieutenant, a sergeant and myself. The rest seemed to have been hit in No Man's Land . . . and the officer said, "Good God, where are the rest of my boys?" but there was nobody left to answer.' Some men broke through near the Fricourt spur but were beaten back by flame-throwers and almost none made any headway into La Boisselle village. Around the La Boisselle crater fierce fighting had enabled some tenuous footholds to be established on the extreme right, but with no reinforcements and limited ammunition, the Tynesiders were in a bleak situation. Men of the 19th (Western) Division were ordered forward but in the face of such heavy enemy fire it was decided to wait until nightfall.

Meanwhile, the 8th Division had also moved forward, but it too had been

The Mines

Understanding the destructive power of such mines is difficult. Y Sap contained 40,000 lb (18 tonnes) of Ammonal and the La Boisselle crater, some 60,000 lb (27 tonnes). The 'Lochnagar' crater remains to this day the largest surviving man-made crater created in warfare. It is almost 300 feet (91.4m) across and 100 feet (30m) deep and covers an area of 70,695 square feet (6,567.5m2) with a volume of 7,550,000 cubic feet (213,791.3m3). As figures, these are meaningless, but put into context, the 488,800 tons (496,620 tonnes) of chalk displaced is the equivalent weight of six QE2s, or the same amount in tonnage as twenty days of supplies for the entire Allied armies landing on D-Day. The force of the explosion blew debris 4,250 feet (1,295m) into the air, where RFC observers were somewhat surprised to be assaulted by rising lumps of chalk. The explosion was audible in London.

under observation for some time by the Germans, one of whom left a detailed account:

'There could be seen a mass of steel helmets above the parapet showing that the troops were ready for the assault. At 7.30am our men clambered up the steep shafts leading from the dugout to daylight . . . and a rough firing line was thus rapidly established. A few moments later, when the leading British line was within 100 yards [91.4m], the rattle of machine-gunfire and musketry broke out along the whole line. Whole sections seemed to fall . . . the advance rapidly crumpled under this hail of shell and bullets. All along the line men could be seen throwing up their arms and collapsing, never to move again. Again and again the extended lines of British infantry broke against the German defences . . . it was an amazing spectacle of unexampled gallantry.'

Incredibly the remains of two battalions, the 2nd Devonshires and 2nd Middlesex, comprising less than eighty men, managed to capture 300 yards (274.3m) of German trench at La Boisselle, which they held on to for two hours. But it was a lost cause and by afternoon the Germans were once again in possession of their entire front line and between the 8th and 34th Divisions a staggering 11,000 men had become casualties. Such were the numbers of wounded, the Germans allowed an unofficial truce later in the day, to permit stretcher-bearers to remove them. Aside from two slight bulges in the line to the north and south of Ovillers, nothing had been gained.

A cheery group of Royal Artillerymen seated on a pile of what appear to be 60-pounder shells. The goatskin jackets were still widely worn in winter 1916, but proved impractical in the wet weather and were replaced with a lined leather jerkin that was both practical and popular (Royal Armouries).

I July: The Attacks on Fricourt and Mametz

If there was a fulcrum upon which the balance of success for the offensive rested, it was the villages of Fricourt and Mametz. The task of capturing them had been given to XV Corps commander, Lieutenant General Sir Henry Horne. As with the villages further north, they had been built on two projecting spurs, giving the Germans an excellent view and providing a tough obstacle for any attacking force. The defenders had not been idle, building an interlocking series of tunnels and machine-gun posts through the cellars underneath the village that stretched for over 1,200 yards (1km) along the front. If this were not enough, there were also two lines of heavily fortified reserve trenches placed at 3 and 6 miles (4.8 and

1 July: The Attack on Fricourt and Mametz

9.6km) behind the front line. In fact, so strong was the Fricourt line, the attacking division, the 21st (New Army) were ordered to work around the village and cut it off, allowing 'mop-up' troops to then clear it. The 7th (Regular) Division were then given the harder task of taking Mametz, thus enabling the brigades of both divisions to link behind the German lines. One advantage that stood in the favour of the British was that effective counter-battery work by the Royal Artillery had all but destroyed the German artillery positions, so they would not face the level of retaliatory shellfire that had been experienced to the north. A heavy pre-Zero barrage began at 6.25am and at 7.28am three mines of 9,000, 15,000, and 25,000 pounds (4,082kg, 6,804kg, 11,340kg) were detonated under the Tambour strongpoint, situated just in front of Fricourt. The plan called for the men to move forward behind a creeping barrage that in practice did not so much creep as leap ahead of them. Nevertheless, the 20th Manchesters and 1st Royal Welsh Fusiliers made significant gains, penetrating the lines to a depth of some 700 yards (640m) and getting into Mametz. In addition, some elements of the 21st Division managed to gain a foothold to the rear of Fricourt, leaving the German defenders in an increasingly precarious position. Some surrendered promptly, while others – predominantly machine-gunners in reinforced bunkers – continued to fight, causing serious losses. Cruellest of all were the casualties inflicted on the 10th West Yorks Regiment. These troops ran into the enfilade fire of the German Maxims on the north-west edge of Fricourt, losing an unprecedented 710 men: the highest battalion casualties of the day. By midafternoon Mametz was in British hands, the line having advanced a total of 2,500 yards (2.2km). They had driven a wedge into the German lines that threatened to cut off Fricourt, still obstinately holding out. The corps had taken 8,000 casualties, mostly through the determined fire from the German Maxims.

The 9th Devons

Men often predicted their own deaths, but the case of Captain Duncan Lennox Martin of the 9th Devons was particularly unusual. Having seen the plan of attack he was deeply unsettled by many of the details and made a plasticine model of the terrain over which his men would advance. They were to attack a trench known as The Shrine, to the south of Mametz, but he saw that the German machine-gun emplacements in Fricourt Wood would be able to enfilade the attacking troops, which was precisely what happened. Martin and 156 of his men perished in the attack. They were buried in their jumping-off trench, with the legend 'The Devons held this trench. The Devons hold it still.'

Campaign Chronicle

I July: The Fight For Montauban

While the fighting for Fricourt and Mametz was underway, further south XIII Corps, under Lieutenant General Sir E.W. Congreve, was to reap — at least partially — the rewards of the failed attack at Gommecourt, which drew the Germans away from the thrust further south. While Montauban Ridge was defended by no less than nine battalions of German infantry, they were taking a more relaxed approach to the war, not expecting any major assault along their front. Nevertheless, the first two lines of defence contained some tough objectives, among them Pommiers, Glatz, Powder, and Castle Redoubts, but the third line was still being constructed. In addition, German artillery in this sector was minimal and the British guns, with the aid of the French further south, were vastly superior in strength, with a ratio of around four-to-one. These factors gave the British a considerable advantage. Two divisions, the 18th (Eastern) and 30th (New Army) were to provide the thrust of the attacking force, while the 9th (Scottish) would be held in reserve. The men were tired, apprehensive, and heavily laden, as Private C. Jarman, 7th Queens Royal West Surreys later recalled: 'I was carrying 200 rounds of ammunition, and as a bomber, fourteen Mills bombs, as well as my other equipment and we had been

Men occupying a recently captured trench on Thiepval Ridge peer carefully over the parapet. Careless exposure would normally result in a sniper's bullet (Royal Armouries).

36

1 July: The Fight For Montauban

instructed to walk not run. Not that I could have run if I'd wanted to.' As the men slowly advanced the inevitable machine-gunfire swelled up: 'We were simply mown down. I can remember stumbling several times under the weight of all my equipment.' The timing of the British barrage was not perfect, the men finding themselves walking into their own shells: 'You could feel the heat and blast, and red-hot shards of steel went flying past everywhere. I expected to be hit at any second but clenched my jaw and just hoped I'd get through it.'

The men continued to move towards the Castle strongpoint and were soon in the enemy trenches, where in savage trench-by-trench fighting they slowly pushed the Germans back. The Pommiers Redoubt fell, and within an hour the division had captured its objectives. Among the 3,115 casualties was Private Jarman, who received a shell splinter wound that shattered his right shin, eventually resulting in gangrene, for which the only solution was amputation. In some respects he considered himself fortunate, for of the fifteen men in his section, only two emerged alive from the attack.

On their right, the brigades of the 30th Division, containing more Pals Battalions, moved towards Montauban, losing hundreds of men to intense fire from the well entrenched 23rd (2nd Upper Silesian) Infantry's machine-guns. However, by 10am they had entered the village, which to their astonishment, they found empty. Within an hour, the shallow defile behind, known as Montauban Alley, had also fallen to the 16th and 17th Manchesters: this meant the 30th Division had achieved its objectives for the loss of some 3,000 men. To their right, their French allies with their tough XX 'Iron Corps' had also achieved considerable success. Their experience at Verdun was to hold them in good stead, for they knew the British practice of advancing in open order was suicidal, and they had learned to move in short rushes, taking cover when possible. Surprised by the ferocity of the assault, most of the defenders fell back, only the village of Curlu holding out. South of the Somme river another French attack – by the First Colonial and XXXV Divisions – was successful, some 4,000 German being captured. Foch offered to continue his advance, but Haig declined, probably wisely, as the lack of gains to the north of the front meant his left flank was in the air.

There was no escaping the fact the British Army had suffered grievously on the first day. The figures make sad reading: killed, 19,240 officers and men; wounded, 35,393; missing (mostly later confirmed dead) 3,049. A further 585 were captured. The total loss of 57,470 men is the highest for one battle in British history. German dead and wounded for the period up to 1 July are unknown, but probably stood at 7–8,000 men, of whom almost 2,500 were captured. Gains had been almost nil in the northern sector, but some success

Although poor quality, this is a genuine photograph of men of the 7th Division attacking towards Mametz on I July. The flat ground has no shred of cover and it can be easily understood why such attacks were doomed to failure in the face of concentrated defensive machine-gunfire (Imperial War Museum Q86).

had been realized further south. Meanwhile, Fourth Army headquarters was blissfully unaware of the level of casualties or the true tactical situation and ordered a resumption of the offensive next morning. Although nobody yet realized it, the Battle of the Somme had barely begun.

2 July: The Battle Continues

While there was no doubt the fearsome losses sustained on the opening day of the campaign were a setback to Haig's plans, they did not in themselves provide a sound reason for abandoning the whole concept. No one had thought that any assault of this magnitude would be easy, besides there had been some gains, and the battle had begun to develop its own momentum. But

3–4 July: The Fighting for Ovillers and La Boisselle

Haig's policy of relentlessly hammering away at the German defences with frontal assaults had its critics, including the French, whose experiences at Verdun had shown them little was to be accomplished by fighting in this manner – except unacceptable casualties rates. A hasty meeting between Haig and Joffre resulted in deadlock, with the Frenchman insisting that attacks to the *north* of the Albert – Bapaume road be resumed at once, which Haig refused, stating his belief that it was success to the *south* of the road that should be built upon. Despite the high level of casualties it was felt there was a good probability of overwhelming the Germans. Haig was resolute in his belief that continuing to push the enemy hard was the only way to wear him down. He was not entirely wrong, for by the night of 1 July, some German units – in particular vital artillery supports – were close to cracking, due to a combination of exhaustion and lack of supplies. In particular, the entire German trench system between the River Somme and the Amiens road was in chaos, with some major defence lines in Trones and Bernafay Woods abandoned. Had the British been able to exploit this, the outcome of the battle might have been very different, for the woods dotted along the front were to provide the Germans with an almost unbreakable line of defences: destined to claim thousands of lives.

3–4 July: The Fighting for Ovillers and La Boisselle

On 3 July a conference of corps commanders held at Fourth Army headquarters heard Haig reiterating his idea that continuing the battle along the southern sector was the only logical decision to take. There would still be attacks to try to make gains in the north, but the thrust of the campaign was still to be aimed at securing the prominent areas around Hardecourt, capturing the tactically significant Trones and Mametz Woods, as well as making another effort to take Ovillers and the village of Contalmaison. Intelligence reports had suggested the German line between La Boisselle and Hardecourt was thin and only fifteen heavily depleted German battalions were in line. As was subsequently discovered, there were actually thirty-three experienced battalions there, with another forty in reserve. The plan therefore required an attack along the line from Ovillers, south-east to Hardecourt, capturing all the woods between, which would have been daunting enough, but to compound matters, artillery ammunition was in such short supply the French had to loan shells to the Royal Artillery siege batteries.

Corps level assaults were to continue next day, but they were fractured and had none of the impetus required to force a significant breakthrough. Little could be done to renew attacks on the front covered by X and VIII Corps apart

18. Although when out of the line troops were supposed to be resting, few were able to escape the inevitable work parties. Apart from being dangerous, as fatigue parties attracted shellfire, the men resented being used as forced labour. Here tired looking soldiers carry screw-picket posts and wire up the line somewhere on the Somme (Imperial War Museum, C0.1988).

3–4 July: The Fighting for Ovillers and La Boisselle

from reinforcing the battered survivors of the 36th (Ulster) Division at Thiepval and those clinging on in the Liepzig Redoubt. Haig wanted Thiepval kept under continual pressure to help draw off German reserves further south, so he could exploit gains already made. This was little consolation to the troops dug in there, who suffered from heavy shelling and repeated German counter-attacks. Thus 3 July saw a resumption of the battle for the Ovilliers–La Boisselle lines on III and X Corps' front. By sheer determination some attacking battalions of the 12th Division reached the German lines at Ovillers but were overwhelmed once they entered the maze of trenches around the village. By late morning they had suffered 2,400 casualties. Things went marginally better for the 19th Division at La Boisselle, which managed to capture the entire village. A series of minor battles then erupted between German and British units, which ebbed and flowed around what little remained of the shattered buildings. At the end of the day the attackers had been forced back and the total gains could be measured in dozens of yards. Yet another attack was launched on the Leipzig Redoubt, by the 32nd Division, but it achieved little except the loss of over 1,000 men.

But an assault by the 17th Division of XV Corps, whose mixed Territorial units attacked Fricourt, and an assault by the 21st Division on their left flank, proved successful. Meanwhile III Corps, using the battalions of the 19th Division, resumed attacks on the village of La Boisselle, now horribly carpeted with dead. The men of the 13th Rifle Brigade were tasked with burying those that lay within the British lines before disease broke out, and the huge mine crater of 'Lochnagar' was the ideal place. Corporal J. Hayles, MM, remembered the smell: 'It was so awful it nearly poisoned you. The old German front line was covered with bodies – they were seven or eight deep and they had all gone black . . . we threw them into that crater, there must have been over a thousand bodies there. I'll never forget it. I was only eighteen, but I thought "there's something wrong here."'

La Boisselle was to be attacked again after a hurricane bombardment at 4pm and the advancing troops, mainly the 6th Wiltshires and 9th Royal Welsh Fusiliers, managed to gain access to the village, linking with the 5th Cheshires on the right. By late evening the western half of the village was in British hands. Elsewhere reserves were sent up to buffer the line at Ovillers and Thiepval. The next few days were spent in consolidating positions, clearing the dead and wounded, reinforcing collapsed trenches, fixing the wire, replenishing stores and ammunition, in particular grenades. On 4 July, to compound the problems already facing the British troops, the weather turned and it began to rain incessantly.

Campaign Chronicle

7–8 July: The Battles for Trones and Mametz Woods

The attacks planned for 7 July took place in high winds and driving rain. To the north, the news was not good for X Corps: German counter-attacks had finally forced the Ulstermen from Thiepval and despite valiant attempts by the grenade men of the Kings Own Yorkshire Light Infantry, they were forced by evening to withdraw to their original lines, the 49th Division having lost many men for no gains. To their right flank, the 25th and 12th Divisions were trying to find a way into the heavily protected Leipzig Redoubt, and along the line of trenches around Ovillers. Incredibly, the 1st Battalion, Wiltshire Regiment, managed to force their way into the redoubt, and aided by excellent artillery support they took the German lines. Alas, the troops advancing into Ovillers had exactly the opposite experience, with a mistimed British bombardment catching them in the open and killing over 300 men: but they doggedly pressed on and by late morning had captured all three German lines. Meanwhile, between Ovillers and Contalmaison, III Corps was given the task of capturing tiny Bailiff Wood, immediately west of Contalmaison. Both the 19th and 23rd Divisions were involved, with the 1st Worcesters reaching the village, only to be driven out by the tough defensive tactics of the 3rd (2nd East Prussian) Grenadier Regiment, who occupied the trenches between the two villages. Three battalions of East Lancashires tried to pick their way through the rain and mud, but came under such heavy fire from Contalmaison they had not the physical strength or numbers to retain their positions or link with units on their flanks. Fortunately, battalions who held the higher ground eventually enabled the scattered groups to make contact and form a loose line with the 19th Division to their left. These attacks, while difficult enough in the conditions, were overshadowed by the objective facing XV Corps: Mametz Wood. The 38th (Welsh) Division led the advance and in the space of seven hours four battalions tried in vain to reach it, driven back each time by intense machine-gunfire from well sited emplacements. Reinforcements from the 17th Division were ordered up but got bogged down in the mud. The attack was eventually called off. This also had an unfortunate knock-on effect, preventing III Corps to their left from advancing on Contalmaison, whose defenders were able to continue pouring machine-gunfire into them. The following day, 8 July, the first attacks were launched on Trones Wood to the east, where the Germans had laid new belts of concealed barbed wire and sited interlocking machine-gun posts, as well as entrenching large numbers of reinforcements. While the infantry of XIII Corps (comprising the 9th and 30th Divisions) formed up in and around Bernafay Wood – one of the few woods in British hands – the French advanced to the south of Hardecourt. The British soldiers left Bernafay Wood

A French 370mm howitzer in the Ravine de Proyart at the southern edge of the Somme. French artillery support was seldom acknowledged but it added to the Allies ability to fight in the southern sector of the front and their heavy howitzers could smash the deepest of dugouts (Musée de l'armée, Belgium).

at 8am and moved towards Trones, the 2nd Wiltshires managing to get some purchase on its very south-eastern edge, while the 9th Division, who were working their way along the eastern side, were driven back by machine-gun and artillery fire. Elsewhere, men dug in and tried to catch some sleep. Private Eastwick of the Wiltshires said of the attack: 'We seemed to have a damn Jerry machine-gun every few yards, our bombers would rush one and another would start up. We kept losing men, one minute they were with you, then they'd be gone. We never got to grips with the machine-gunners, but they'd never have been allowed to surrender, I can tell you that. By afternoon we were quite done in.'

Campaign Chronicle

9–13 July: Further Assaults

From the second week of July a series of further assaults took place on and around Contalmaison, with the aim of securing both the village and the woods to the east. Mercifully, the weather had improved and the 9th was cloudy but dry, and frankly, the assaulting troops of III, XV and XIII Corps needed all the help they could get. Probably the toughest nut to crack was still Mametz, once again the focus of the 38th Welsh Division. They advanced at first light, 4.15am, behind a short bombardment, which it was hoped would not alert the Germans. Three battalions of Welsh Fusiliers (14th, 15th and 16th) supported by one of the Welsh Regiment reached the edge of the wood where the fighting became intense, bloody and confused. The wood itself was to become a byword for the worst savagery and carnage of modern warfare. Lieutenant Wyn Griffith of the 15th Welsh Fusiliers was at the centre of the assault and in his seminal book on the battle wrote:

> 'Years of neglect had turned the wood into a formidable barrier, a mile deep. Heavy shelling of the southern end had . . . thrown trees and large branches into a barricade. There were more corpses than men, but there were worse sights. Limbs and mutilated trunks, here and there a detached head, formed vivid splashes of red against the green leaves and as in an advertisement of the horror of our way of life, one tree held in its branches a leg, with its torn flesh hanging down over a spray of leaf.'

After almost twelve hours fighting, the 38th had got to within 40 yards (36.5m) of the northern edge of the wood, but were stopped by heavy machine-gunfire. Meanwhile, the 17th Division had captured Contalmaison after using grenades to bomb the Germans out, and the West Yorks and Green Howards of the 23rd Division were successful in forcing back the Germans to the edge of Bailiff Wood, just to the west of the village. Casualties had been heavy: the 9th Green Howards being reduced to five officers and 150 men. As for the battered 38th Division, who were still fighting to keep their foothold in Mametz, relief could not come too soon, and on the morning of the 12th they were eventually relieved by men of the 12th Division. Lieutenant Griffith was among the few who stumbled out, leaving behind his brother, whose body was never found. He later wrote: 'The dead were chosen, and Fate had forgotten us in its eager clutching at the men who fell: they were the richer prize. They captured Mametz Wood, and in it they lie.'

Meanwhile, on that same day, General von Falkenhayn put and end to the Verdun offensive, releasing yet more troops to assist on the Somme.

The pressure was to be kept up on the Germans, however, and the 30th Division were still battering away at Trones Wood, but the men were exhausted

44

Unlike their German counterparts, British front-line trenches were never considered to be permanent structures. This is a typical example of a front-line post, with a camouflaged periscope for observation. The wire entanglements are visible on the parapet and though easily defended it was vulnerable to shell-fire (R. Dunning).

and had to be replaced by troops of the 18th Division on 13 July. Mametz fell after a concerted attack by men of the Royal West Kents, Middlesex, and Buffs. Around Contalmaison the battalions of the 23rd Division were steadily working forwards, and after beating off a German counter-attack, succeeded in taking the bricks and cellars that was all that remained of the village: leaving a salient of Germans in a fortified position called Quadrangle Trench. Unsupported on either flank, it too fell, and by the night of the 13th a line had been established north of most of the planned objectives. But Ovilliers remained defiant, despite continued attacks. Between 2–13 July some forty-six small-scale attacks had been launched across the Fourth Army front, which resulted in over 25,000 Allied casualties for no appreciable gains.

Campaign Chronicle

14–31 July: Battles for the Bazentin and Longueval Ridges

Even as British troops were still fighting to gain control of the woods around Contalmaison, events were underway at GHQ that it was better they did not know about. General Rawlinson had already held a meeting with brigade commanders to discuss the future strategy of the campaign, and it was decided a new assault should be delivered on a line stretching from Longueval to Bazentin-le-Petit. Thus XIII Corps would front the attack, while the divisions under XV Corps would launch simultaneous attacks on Bazentin-le-Grand Wood and its village, using the cover of their hard-won trenches in Mametz Wood. On the far left III Corps was to undertake a flank attack to keep the

These Germans are ensconced in a deep dugout, protected not only from the incessant shelling, but also the elements. A china oil-lamp, beer and wine are on the table, a field telephone sits on the wall and a sniping rifle and flare pistol hang on the wooden boarded wall behind the man on the left. It was little wonder that German soldiers became reluctant to leave such protection (Bundesarchiv).

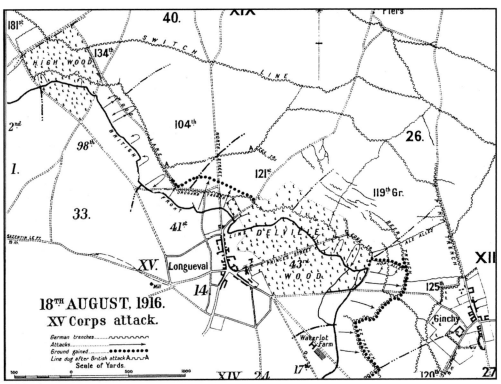

The attack on High Wood and Delville Wood, 18 August.

Germans occupied. Yet there were doubts about the plan's viability: the French were concerned their British allies would be unable to prevent enemy observers spotting their preparations. But the bombardment began regardless on the 11th, concentrating on the areas around High Wood, Flers, Martinpuich, Le Sars and Bapaume. The infantry assault was to start at 3.25am on the 14th, while it was still dark. This, it was hoped, would prevent German machine-gunners from firing effectively, giving the attackers a better chance of reaching the wire unscathed.

Once again it was the heavily defended woods that were the focus of the fighting, with Delville, High, Bazentin-le-Petit and Leuze Woods all yet to be captured, along with their associated villages, Longueval and Martinpuich, which stretched along a geographical feature known as Bazentin Ridge. At dawn, the 8th (Scottish) Division advanced on the south-west edge of Delville Wood and managed to take it, continuing after some hard fighting to secure most of Longueval by 10am. The 3rd Division did not have an easy time, for on reaching the enemy lines they found the wire mostly intact and it took a spirited assault by some of the 2nd Royal Scots, who crossed the wire and bombed their way along the trench, to enable the other battalions to get into the lines. The 7th Division, to the right of Mametz Wood, had two-thirds of a mile (1km) of No Man's Land to cross, so their commander sensibly moved them to within 300 yards (274.3m) of the German trenches under cover of darkness, and at 3.45am they successfully stormed the trenches in front of them. Bazentin-le-Grand Wood was attacked an hour later by 20th Brigade and they were able to secure it, the Royal Irish Regiment clearing the village with bomb and bayonet. Private T. Williams of the Royal Irish Regiment recalled: 'We moved from one pile of rubble to another and dropped bombs into the cellars and dugouts. We had suffered badly and they got little mercy from our boys. I saw three of our men bayoneting a machine-gun crew who tried to surrender.' Some 2,000 German prisoners were taken and their casualties were high. While no reliable figures exist for the battle, British casualties amounted to about 9,000 men and the Germans losses were double that. So successful was the attack that for the first time, cavalry was sent forward, to the amusement of some muddy

Tommies, consolidating their positions: 'On ye go chum!' shouted one Scot, 'We've doon all the bluidy hard work for ye.'

From late morning however, the initiative began to slip through the fingers of the corps commanders. Incredibly, as the advance continued to gather momentum, it was discovered that High Wood was devoid of Germans, yet frantic requests from officers at the front to put men into it were refused: a decision the British would soon pay for dearly. An inaccurate report that Longueval had been taken resulted in the 7th Brigade being sent forwards up the bare slope towards High Wood, which sadly was by then no longer empty. Colonel G. Seton-

Men of the Kings Own Regiment wait to move up the line. Their Lewis guns feature prominently and their rifles are early MkI Long Lee-Enfields, which seldom feature in contemporary photographs. The man centre left is unaccountably holding up a box of 250 Wills cigarettes! (R. Dunning).

Hutchinson, whose Machine-Gun Corps battalion was providing covering fire from trenches near Bazentin, had a grandstand view of the attack:

> 'I, looking across the valley . . . could see the men of the 1st Queens passing up the slope to Martinpuich. Suddenly they wavered and a few of the foremost attempted to cross some obstacles in the grass. They were

awkwardly lifting their legs over a low wire entanglement. Some two hundred men, their commander at their head had been brought to a standstill at this point. A scythe seemed to cut their feet from under them and the line crumpled and fell, stricken by machine-gunfire. Those in support wavered . . . there was no shred of cover, and they fell in their tracks, as rabbits fall at a shooting battue.'

By early evening only a small part of High Wood was in British hands and the Germans had by then returned in strength. Tragically, the corps commander of the British troops who had managed to enter High Wood mistakenly ordered their retreat, allowing the mystified Germans to advance and occupy the trenches once again. The other main sticking point for the advancing British was proving to be the dominant green mass of Delville Wood, which the South African Brigade, serving with the 9th (Scottish) Division, had managed to fight their way into, having first fought through the ruins of Longueval and the heavily defended area of Waterlot Farm. Delville proved too tough even for them, and their entry was stopped abruptly by a monumental German bombardment.

Further west, the irritating defenders of Ovillers were still managing to hold out against artillery bombardment, gas and repeated attacks by X Corps. But eventually the garrison's morale cracked, and white-faced, blinking Germans emerged from their dugouts and cellars, waving white cloths. By the morning of the 17th the village was finally in British hands. At Poziers, the ANZAC forces were ordered to relieve the tired men of the Fourth Army. As Delville was to become synonymous with the South African sacrifice on the Somme, so too would Poziers with the ANZACs. The following day a conference was held at GHQ to discuss the objectives of the Fourth Army, to bring some order to the confusing and often fluid front line. It was decided that XV Corps should try to take High Wood on the 20th, with a simultaneous assault on Delville Wood and Longueval by XIII Corps, which would attack as far as the Somme river with the assistance of the French infantry to their right. On the morning of 20 July, the 5th, 7th, and 33rd Divisions of XV Corps set out to try — once again — to drive the Germans from High Wood. The weather was hot and the stench from the thousands of unburied bodies hung over the area like a pall. There were some bizarre sights, as Rifleman J. Brown, 16th KRRC recalled: 'On the way up there was a trench at right angles to where we was and it was full of dead Germans, just standing where they'd been shot. You could see their heads and shoulders . . . they hadn't fallen down and they'd gone as black as pitch.' After continual shelling, the wood had become a shattered, splintered nightmare of intertwined tree roots, branches and shell holes. After a few yards men became

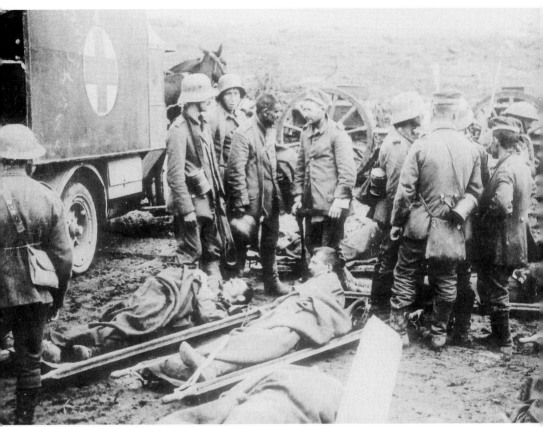

As casualties mounted it became imperative to remove them from the front line as quickly as possible. German prisoners were often used to assist, and many performed beyond the call of duty under heavy shellfire. Under the rules of war, officers could not be asked to undertake such menial tasks but more than one veteran recalled using a bayonet to gain compliance (Author's collection).

hopelessly disorientated and it was a sniper's paradise: the Germans took a steady toll of British Tommies. The attacking battalions entered the wood and a hail of machine-gun and rifle fire that drove the men of the 33rd Division back to their starting point. Neither were the South Africans faring well in Delville Wood. They had entered it with 121 officers and 3,032 other ranks, and left it with twenty-one officers and 751 other ranks. So heavy was the artillery fire poured in, that it was impossible to find shelter and several brigade commanders began to think that bypassing it might be a wiser course of action.

Nowhere along the front were any of the attacking divisions able to make headway, and this was mainly due to poor communication, resulting in part from inadequate staff coordination and planning. Attacks had been timed for

Stretcher-bearers carry a grimacing wounded man back to an aid post on the Somme. In dry conditions two men could manage a stretcher but it was hard work. When the weather deteriorated, in the cloying mud eight men were often needed, working in relays (R. Dunning).

different Zero Hours, artillery units were given conflicting orders, and preparation was nowhere near as effective as it should have been. On the 22nd Rawlinson ignored the pleas of the French, who insisted they were not yet in a position to attack, and demanded his plans be adhered to. The fighting was not one-sided however, for the defenders had fared equally badly. The constant shelling and repeated attacks had cost them dearly. The German division holding Delville Wood lost at least 9,500 men: a significantly higher casualty rate than at Verdun. Still the attacks continued on Longueval, High Wood and along the Hardecourt-Guillemont line. There had been four previously unsuccessful attacks on the village and windmill at Pozières, which held a commanding position overlooking Thiepval. But on 23 July the 48th (South Midland) and the 1st Australian Divisions launched an all-out midnight assault under cover of an effective artillery barrage and succeeded in capturing the village. This was a significant success, in which two Australian soldiers won the Victoria Cross. Capturing it of course was one thing, holding onto it was another. By the final day of the month the temperature had soared, and the battlefield was black with clouds of huge flies. Meanwhile, giant rats feasted on the dead. Little ground had been gained and the German strongpoints continued to dominate the landscape. Their names were becoming depressingly familiar to the soldiers: Beaumont Hamel, Thiepval, Martinpuich, Longueval and Guillemont.

1–18 August: The Attacks on Pozières, Guillemont, and Maurepas

The month of August was to be characterized by a series of piecemeal attacks along virtually the whole front and it was significant for several reasons. First, it had become obvious to GHQ that without meticulous planning closely involving the divisional artillery, any further attacks were going to be doomed to costly failure. Second, Haig began to realize the German Army was not yet on its knees and was likely to continue fighting tenaciously for control of the ground. Third, at home there was increasing public disquiet as the casualty lists of sons, brothers, and fathers grew ever longer for little or no gain.

To feed the insatiable demand for men, each day 1,000 soldiers were required, and these had to be transferred from base camps to the front line to replace the casualties. Many were not trained to the standards normally required, some having had only the most basic shooting instruction on their rifles. Marksmanship, which had been the cornerstone of the Regular Army, was now considered of little consequence. The few old soldiers still serving in line battalions shuddered at the lack of ability shown by the new arrivals. It was not simply their shooting ability that was in question, GHQ even doubted their discipline, and there was considerable worry at corps level that the recruits would not perform well in battle. In practice such concerns proved almost entirely misplaced, and despite the hammering the army had received, the war-weariness of 1917 and 1918 had not yet imbued the men of 1916. True, they were tired, and many were beginning to suffer from what is now known as battle fatigue or Post-Traumatic Stress Disorder. This was a combination of exhaustion, fear and uncertainty that took its toll on the nerves and some men inevitably cracked under the pressure. At the time, it was simply referred to as 'funk'. Generally though, morale was good and grim humour was always on tap. As Lieutenant J. Hayward of the Royal Berkshires marched reinforcements up to the line, one Royal Engineer wag shouted from a dugout: 'Look after 'em sir, 'cos we can't keep up with the demand for crosses.'

Forward artillery observation posts became increasingly important to enable officers to direct the fire of their guns accurately. Many Forward Observation Officers accompanied attacking troops to ensure they could report to their batteries as quickly as possible, although communications were always diffi-cult. This one is too prominently placed to be close to the front line (R. Dunning).

For the first week, action along the front mostly took the form of local attacks to try to capture the many strongpoints still held by the Germans. The troops holding on to footholds in Longueval and Delville Woods were relieved, but an attempt made by XV and III Corps to advance their lines in front of Martinpuich, Delville, and High Woods met with failure. On the 7th, the 2nd ANZAC Division launched a large-scale assault on the Pozières Windmill and it took four separate waves of infantry to force the strongpoint. A successful follow-up was marred by poor planning when, a week later, the 2nd Australian Division, which had relieved the 1st, attacked the ground between the village and its heavily fortified windmill, losing 3,500 men in the process. Having consolidated their position in what was now nothing more than a shell-pocked wasteland, the ANZACs had to fight off three desperate German counter-attacks.

Sitting midway between Pozières, Courcelette, and Thiepval, the fortified strongpoint called Mouquet Farm (universally referred to as 'Mucky' or 'Moo-Cow' Farm) still held out and on 9 August the Australian 1st, 2nd, and 4th Divisions began repeated assaults in the area, but they were hampered by a narrow frontage, which made retaliatory German artillery fire particularly effective, as any shells that came over were more or less guaranteed to find a target. The bloody battles for Mouquet Farm were to continue for almost a month and ANZAC losses would surpass 23,000 men.

Guillemont, with Ginchy nestling behind it, had a series of German strongpoints that ran roughly south from the edge of Delville Wood, where a fortified area called Waterlot Farm protected the gap between the wood and the village. These lines ran past Guillemont to the boundary of the Anglo-French lines near Hardecourt and the River Somme. They protected the extreme flank of the battle area and had forced the French into a bottleneck, preventing them from moving forward. General Fayolles, commanding, was desperate for a British attack on Guillemont and Ginchy to free his troops. As Haig believed, in his own words, that he must 'help the French forward', a heavy bombardment was begun and the 2nd and 55th Divisions were launched to the attack. It was to be a depressingly similar story to the ill-starred attack on Serre some weeks before. Once more, the British artillery barrage moved forward too quickly. permitting the Germans to reoccupy their positions. The 1/4th Kings Own were held up by wire and caught by machine-guns, but the 1/8th Kings Own (Liverpool Irish) fought their way forward and managed to get into the village. Next day the attacks were renewed with 55th Division again at the sharp end of the fighting with a dawn assault led by the Kings Liverpool Scottish and the Loyal North Lancs, but they too met with fearsome machine-gun and shellfire. Neither were the 2nd Division any more successful: the 17th Middlesex Regiment got to within bombing range of the village but were forced back. Private G. Waters recalled: 'We went through awful machine-gunfire, the bullets were buzzing past like swarms of bees and I kept thinking "I'll stop one any minute." But we got to the edge of the village, which was a shambles and took cover in some shell holes. Our sergeant threw some bombs, but any movement attracted a storm of gunfire and we decided to stay put until we could get back.' Eventually, under cover of darkness, the few who had made it to their objective slipped back to their lines and counted their luck.

Apart from casualties, the forward troops were also suffering from shortages of both water and ammunition. The Germans had used saturation bombardment along the British front to great effect, emulating the British artillery's pummelling of their lines pre-1 July. Day and night they traversed their artillery along every inch of the front and rear areas. Men, rations, and ammunition limbers were frequently blown to smithereens before they could reach their dropping off points. And in the August heat lack of water became a serious problem, much of the supply relying on refilled fuel tins carried up by ration parties, which despite washing out, always provided water that tasted of petrol. Men resorted to robbing the dead of their canteens and at least one group happily found themselves with a sergeant's canteen full of rum. Food was scarce too, although with the prevailing stench from unburied dead and swarms of flies, few thought of eating much.

Work continued apace to extend and connect the existing lines and on 11 August, as the temperature mercifully dropped, XV Corps launched yet another

Cavalry move up on a duckboard track past some bemused looking infantry who are resting with their loads of petrol tins. The cavalry never had the chance to break through to open country that they were expecting on the Somme and many ended up fighting as dismounted infantrymen (R. Dunning).

push against High Wood, with the 34th Division managing to gain some 200 yards (182.8m) of enemy lines. Whether this was worth the casualties inflicted is a moot point, but by now any success was considered worthwhile.

Meanwhile, there were continuing problems with the French alliance, for while Haig and Foch had agreed the two armies cooperate to force a passage through Guillemont, Foch was still unhappy at what he saw as Haig's and Rawlinson's piecemeal attacks. He favoured a single massive assault using several divisions along the whole front from Delville Wood southwards. After considerable debate it was agreed that a large-scale attack could be launched on the 18th, along the Guillemont–Maurepas line. Massing of supplies and troops began in earnest, but on the 14th the weather broke suddenly with almost 3mm of rain, setting the scene for the following days. By the end of the month the area would be turned into a huge swamp that dramatically reduced the ability of soldiers to fight. Still, by midmonth, the British III, XIV and XV Corps were ready to attack alongside the French.

Yet the Germans were having their own problems. The fighting on the Eastern Front had proved prolonged and bloody, and the demand for men was becoming greater than even the German Army could sustain. Much to General von Falkenhayn's fury, five divisions of battle-hardened troops were ordered to leave

A typical result of intense shelling, most Somme villages were reduced to little more than brick dust. This made attacking them even more difficult as the defenders dugouts and cellars were protected by tons of rubble. This is the remains of Thiepval Château (Imperial War Museum Q1328).

1–8 August: The Attacks on Pozières, Guillemont, and Maurepas

the Somme for Russia: they were replaced with unseasoned troops comprising reservists and returned wounded, incapable of fierce fighting. Unsurprisingly, von Falkenhayn demanded the immediate return of his seasoned troops. But by August the German Army was nowhere near as strong as it appeared, and the constant harassment by British artillery had made movement of men and supplies doubly difficult. Indeed, one senior German officer reported that he believed the British artillery superior in accuracy and effectiveness to that of his own, adding and that effective target observation, aided by the Royal Flying Corps, meant the British wasted far fewer shells. Had Haig and Foch known, this information would doubtless have heartened them and might possibly have moved Haig to be more amenable to Foch's demands for one massive push.

18–31 August: The Attacks on Martinpuich and High Wood

On 18 August III Corps was occupying lines slightly to the east of the Albert–Bapaume road, alongside the ANZAC Corps and opposite Martinpuich, with High Wood to their extreme right. The Zero Hour for the III Corps attack was 2.45pm but because of mistiming by the covering artillery the 2nd Brigade of the 1st Division walked slap into the British barrage. Unfortunately, it was devastatingly accurate and all but wiped out four battalions, and a similar fate befell the men in the 8th Royal Berkshire. Despite terrible losses, the 1st

Campaign Chronicle

Northampton Regiment stormed the trenches in the north-western edge of High Wood and routed the defenders, the 181st (15th Saxon) Infantry. On either side of the Albert–Bapaume road the ANZAC forces were advancing slowly towards Mouquet Farm and had even managed to take some trenches beyond the Leipzig Redoubt, but the cost was high. The Australians were to lose 23,000 men in six weeks: more than their casualties for the Gallipoli campaign. Unlucky XV Corps had been given the job of driving the Germans from High Wood. At 2.45pm, as the battalions of the 14th Division moved forward, a rain of shells crashed down on them, breaking up their formations. But they plodded on, into the face of the inevitable machine-gunfire. By now the soldiers had learned their lesson, and as the guns traversed, they dropped into cover to let the bullets slash overhead, rising and moving forwards as the Maxim's muzzles moved away. There was little they could do about the rifle fire though. Lance Corporal E. Gale of the 7th Rifle Brigade was in the cover of a shell hole with his sergeant, who incautiously raised his head to see what the attacking troops were doing, only to receive a bullet in the ear: 'It blew half his face away. Me and Jack had to lay there with him.' When Gale crawled back at dusk dragging a wounded officer with him, he had had enough of soldiering: 'It was a miracle any of us got back. I don't believe I ever cried in my life, but when I got back and found out what had happened, how many men we'd lost, I cried then.' Twenty-three men had survived of his original company. To the right of High Wood, the 33rd Division were also having a difficult time, for while the 1/4th Suffolks had reached the first German line they were unable to push further forward and even the tough 2nd Argyll and Sutherland Highlanders were unable to press home their attack, eventually being forced to retreat.

Meanwhile, XIV Corps had simultaneously launched its bid to oust the Germans and break the deadlock by taking the hitherto impregnable village of Guillemont. To the north of their line, bordering Delville Wood, 3rd Division's 8th Royal West Kents had bombed their way into the German lines, enabling a slight gain to be made in the trenches behind Waterlot Farm and opposite Ginchy, from where they linked with the extreme flank elements of XV Corps 14th Division. Further south of Guillemont, things were not so rosy, for the casualties caused by the machine-guns of the German 123rd (5th Württemberg) Grenadier Regiment had inflicted heavy losses on the 1st Northumberland Fusiliers, and had forced them to abandon their advance. This led to a domino effect: for their withdrawal left the British flank wide open and the Welsh Fusiliers to one side, and East Yorks on the other, had to fall back as well. A little south of the village, the 24th Division had also fallen foul of the Württembergers' machine-guns, but they made some headway, and with help

A wounded German is pulled from the cellar of a house, assisted by his comrades and a British soldier. Clearing out cellars and dugouts became a specialized operation involving close teamwork and the use of many grenades. Both the Scottish and Australian troops excelled at it (R. Dunning).

from the 3rd Rifle Brigade, they dug in for the night, having been able to capture some of the Hardecourt–Guillemont road. The day ended with nothing much achieved in the way of a serious advance. Once again the British and Commonwealth troops had, at considerable cost, merely nibbled away at the edge of the German lines. But Haig was apparently satisfied with results. He wrote in his diary for the 19 August: 'The operation carried out yesterday was most successful. We now hold the ridge south-east of and overlooking Thiepval. Nearly 500 prisoners were taken, while the battalion which carried out the attack lost only forty men.' This was true, but overall casualties for the day were around 6,500 men, and the weather was worsening. The following day saw little in the way of fighting, with relief being carried out and trenches consolidated, but conditions were becoming awful. The heavy chalk soil collected around the men's boots and formed a solid ball weighing 7 or 8 pounds (3 or 3.6kg) on each foot, making walking hard work. According to Private G. Irons of the 12th Middlesex: 'It would take us two or three hours to do maybe 400 yards [365.7m] and by the time we reached our trenches we was exhausted, too tired to keep proper guard. Men fell asleep standing up and our officers was forever prodding sentries to wake them up. They could have been court-martialled but they (the officers) knew how deadbeat we was.'

The period from 19 to 21 August was primarily one of consolidation, with relief of battle weary units. In III Corps, the 25th Division replaced the 49th, while in XIV Corps, the 3rd Division was relieved by the 35th. However, the ANZAC Division to the north of the British line continued to pile the pressure on the Germans holding the trenches opposite Mouquet Farm. The 12th Battalion, South-West Australians and Tasmanians actually managed to force the Germans out of the front line and bombed and bayoneted their way along it, but they were too few and too badly supported to sustain such an action. On the following day the tired ANZACs of the 1st Division were relieved and the 2nd Division took over their trenches. The rest of the month was to see a series of localised assaults on specific strongpoints, all with a similar theme to them. After a brief artillery barrage, troops would move rapidly toward their objectives, into inescapable machine-gunfire, and the level of casualties inflicted makes the pursuit of such tactics seem utterly futile. On the 23rd August, the 20th Divisions' Kings Royal Rifles were beaten back by rifle and machine-gun fire, the same happening with 48th Divisions' 1/1st and 1/4th Ox and Bucks. On the following day III Corps' 1st Division lost many seasoned men from the 2nd Royal Munster Fusiliers. Yet the fighting ability of the men, who were becoming used to German tactics was beginning to pay off, as close examination shows some gains made, which over time allowed the British to extend their lines.

At Delville Wood on the 25th the 14th Division of XV Corps moved up under a creeping barrage, which was timed to perfection, and the Kings Royal Rifle Corps, with the Ox and Bucks Light Infantry, managed to force their way into

An officer and crew of the Heavy Branch Machine-gun Corps, with their 'female' tank. Packing eight men into such a confined space was not easy. The small sponsons of the 'female' are clearly visible to the left, as is the tiny exit hatch beneath it. If the tank caught fire, only the nimblest crew members would be able to escape (Tank Museum, Bovington).

the shattered remains of the wood, where crucially, they linked with outposts of the 33rd Division, holding trenches on the edge of the Flers road. The opposing 72nd (Thuringen) Infantry fought hard to retain their positions but were forced to retire. The 26th saw further attacks by the ANZAC Division, allied to an assault by the men of III Corps, who pushed further into Martinpuich. The Colonial soldiers once more managed to breach the strongpoint of Mouquet Farm, but were mostly captured after losing direction in the featureless wasteland the area had become: although one small post was established that continued to hold out. Elsewhere along the line the ANZAC attacks were less successful: a scene that was to be repeated on the 28th, after considerable losses were inflicted by skilfully situated Maxim guns, catching the Colonials in the flank. The misery of the weather continued too, with an average rainfall of 8mm (0.3 inches) on most days. Tracks became quagmires, duckboards floated away, and trenches flooded, becoming uninhabitable. Private A. Dixon, a Royal Engineer, found it impossible to keep pace with the gradual deterioration of the trenches:

> 'As fast as we shored up a parapet, another big lump would collapse. We couldn't use lorries or even horses to bring supplies of timber or sandbags up, they just sunk so it all had to be hand carried. We were often begged by men to stop and get some poor devil out of a shell hole. Some had sunk almost up to their necks and were in a terrible state so we'd use ropes and planks to get them out. We weren't supposed to stop, but we always did. You had to.'

The final days of August saw little major action, except on XV Corps' front, along Delville Wood, where the 24th Divisional troops suffered a sudden counter-attack by the Germans, which drove them back. But for the most part, the British line held and the enemy advance was checked. The weary ANZACs were replaced by the 1st Canadian Division and the troops in the sodden trenches huddled in the rain, oblivious to the silent entry of September.

A bogged 'male' tank identifiable by its long 6-pounder gun. In the early months of the war the length of the gun proved to be a problem, so armourers lopped almost two feet off it, which despite dire warnings, did not affect its accuracy at all. The smoke blackened door indicates that it has caught fire, the most common fate of tanks hit by shellfire (Tank Museum, Bovington).

1 September: The Ancre Offensive

Although pleased with the limited objectives gained, Haig was frustrated at having failed to break the German lines. He called a conference of commanders to discuss the situation. At the current rate of advance, using piecemeal attacks, it was looking doubtful if by the New Year any significant progress could be measured. As it was, the British advances in August had dented the enemy's lines, but Haig was determined the German defences must be breached before winter set in. To this end, he decided to launch a three-phase attack, using the infantry of the Reserve Army to drive the Germans off the Bazentin Ridge. While the Reserve Army consolidated their gains, the troops of the Fourth Army were to attack along the Albert–Bapaume road as far as Flers. The third phase was to employ Haig's beloved cavalry to push through the gaps made by the infantry. To enable this to happen however, there remained the thorny problem of how to destroy the German wire, and despite much opposition from senior officers, Haig was confident that a British secret weapon, the tank, was just the machine to do it.

The problem facing Haig was that in August there were still insufficient vehicles or trained crews to make up an effective combat force that could be used to batter though the German lines. At the earliest it would be mid-September before sufficient numbers of tanks arrived at the front to assist the attacking force. But it was believed there was a good chance of breaking the German line at Guillemont and Ginchy if a corps level attack was launched without delay, and so the long-suffering XIV and XV Corps were given the job. At Delville Wood, and to the north-west of Ginchy, it was XV Corps' job to gain control of the area, with XV Corps opposite Ginchy. At the top section

---

The Big Secret

So secretive was British High Command about the development of their secret weapon that during its trials at Hatfield Park, the estates workers were moved from their cottages and an army cordon thrown around the entire area. Vehicles leaving the Foster's Factory at Lincoln had no sponsons fitted and were marked on their sides with: 'Water Tanks for Russia'. And so the new weapon got its name. As vehicles were initially not available, troops who had volunteered for the new service were trained in manoeuvring and tactics by carrying around plywood and canvas mock-ups. One veteran recalled that he and his comrades were laughing so hard they steered their 'tank' into a ditch and were incapable of extricating it.

---

of the line, around Thiepval, II Corps was to try to take the infamous Schwaben Redoubt, north and west of Thiepval village.

For the defending Germans, the constant fighting was taking its toll, with the average casualties suffered by each division in August being over 4,500 men, and it was becoming increasingly difficult to replace them with troops of the same calibre. It had also become obvious to the German commanders the almost ceaseless British artillery fire was causing their soldiers not only physical but also psychological problems, making them reluctant to leave the safety of their deep shelters. This was more pronounced with the replacement troops, who were not inured to shellfire. Von Falkenhayn took note of comments by his commanders and it was decided that in future front-line trenches would be sparsely held by seasoned 'caretaker' companies, and a powerful reserve line – later to be better known as the Hindenberg Line – was to be reinforced and occupied by the battalions that had been taken out of the line. The front-line units were also to be reinforced with eleven new divisions formed specifically to man the new Somme defences. As Haig planned his Ancre offensive, the Germans, unbeknown to British intelligence, gradually began to implement this directive and units fell back to the Hindenberg line.

The battle began at 5.10am on 3 September, in heavy rain, with II Corps advancing from St Pierre Divion alongside the River Ancre, to Thiepval. Despite good artillery support and a successful advance into the German trenches, the Wiltshires, Worcesters, and South Lancashire Regiments of the 25th Division were simply not strong enough to retain their newly won positions, and after hard trench fighting they had to withdraw. At 5.13am the 49th Division moved forward along the Thiepval–Hamel road, behind a brief barrage that included gas shells. The men of the 1/4th and 1/5th Duke of Wellington's Regiment managed to take over the enemy's front line in front of the Schwaben Redoubt but to their flank, the supporting troops failed to take their objective, leaving the 'Dukes' open to enfilade fire. Despite this setback, the West Yorkshire Regiment made valiant efforts to reach its objectives. Heavy machine-gun fire from the Schwaben Redoubt didn't help matters, and later in the morning a counter-attack forced out the British units: so by 11am the Germans were back in control. To their right, along the Ancre, V Corps' 39th Division had mixed success, with four battalions of Royal Sussex and Hampshires firmly establishing themselves in the front line, but the valley, with its glutinous mud and flooded trenches, was hard going for the attacking troops, and the slow-moving men became easy targets for the Maxim guns.

Further south, III Corps' attack was launched at 11.59 and thirty seconds by the explosion of a 3,000 lb (1,360kg) mine under the German lines to the left

A tank crew pose with two Lewis guns and their section officer somewhere in France. Initially adopted in 1916 against the wishes of the crews, the Lewis was a poor choice as its voluminous cooling jacket allowed bullets to enter the cabin. Eventually it was replaced by the more suitable Hotchkiss light machine-gun (Author's collection).

edge of High Wood, the crater being rushed by a storming-party of the 1st Black Watch. Faced with hundreds of yelling Scotsmen, those Germans still capable of coherent thought sensibly abandoned their positions and the Scottish troops seized the crater. Unfortunately, they couldn't hold on to it, being forced to abandon the ground after a heavy counter-attack at 3pm. Later that afternoon, the South Wales Borderers, Welch, and Munster Regiments managed to get through the wood, but by nightfall they too had withdrawn, unable to prevent the Germans from infiltrating and bombing them out. The

Campaign Chronicle

ANZACs of 48th Division once more advanced with the objective of taking Mouquet Farm and its surrounding trenches, and this time the 51st and 52nd Battalions took control of the strongpoint. Heavy fighting went on all day and the Australians were reinforced late in the afternoon by fresh Canadian troops, who barricaded the trenches and established a relatively cohesive line. The XV Corps had attacked the south-east edge of Delville Wood, and along the Longueval–Ginchy road at 11.15am, heavy enfilade machine-gunfire made advance difficult: the attackers resorting to storm troop tactics by using small parties to advance in short rushes, shell hole by shell hole. The Royal Welsh Fusiliers excelled at this, and they took the trenches to the immediate west of Ginchy. Some reached the village itself but were annihilated. However, the Manchester and Warwickshire Regiments were able to hold on to their gains on the edge of Ginchy. To their left, the battalions of 24th Division had advanced beyond Delville Wood and established posts beyond it. They then began to link with troops on their right to form a solid line.

It was left to XIV Corps to try to take Guillemont, and in this they were supported by the French 127th Regiment to their right. The King's Own Scottish Borderers attacked south of the village straight into an intense machine-gun barrage and lost over 300 men, while the French suffered likewise. To their left, the 12th Gloucesters and 1st Duke of Cornwall's Light Infantry advanced, and at midday they were reinforced by the 14th and 15th Battalions of the Royal Warwickshire Regiment. At the extreme south of the village the 20th Division, using reserves brought up for the task, assaulted the trenches and engaged in bloody fighting with the tenacious defenders. Lieutenant O'Sullivan of the 6th Connaught Rangers left a graphic account of the attack in his diary:

> 'They went over the top with a rush. On the ridge we were greeted by a hurricane of machine-gun bullets . . . by a lucky miracle the Bosche fire was aimed too high otherwise no one would have escaped. Once more on their feet, the men recovered the wild abandon of the charge just as the Germans began to emerge . . . One group put up hectic resistance, but was overwhelmed by the bayonet stabbing onslaught – then the Irishmen rushed on ahead leaving the crumpled bodies in a stink of blood and high explosive.'

The Hardecourt road was reached with the 7th Leinsters clearing the remaining Germans from the village. Reserves were ordered into Guillemont at 5.30pm to help consolidate. For the next three days, attacks were launched aimed at linking outlying units and capturing remaining strongpoints. Between Combles

1 September: The Ancre Offensive

and Guillemont, Falfemont Farm was finally taken by the 5th Division and the 20th Division managed to consolidate their positions in Leuze Wood, west of Combles. Finally, the outposts between Guillemont and Leuze Wood were joined and a rough line was formed. All this was done, not only in the face of heavy shelling and machine-gun fire, but on a day where 25mm (0.9 inches) of rain fell. The 7 and 8 September were used to move up reinforcement to replace worn-out units, but the best news for all the men huddled in their waterlogged dugouts was that it finally stopped raining. Early in the evening of the 8th, III Corps launched a lightening attack on High Wood, meeting with some limited success, but they had to be withdrawn by midnight. The 9th was to see the eventual fall of Ginchy, as the 56th and 16th Divisions of XIV Corps attacked at 4.45pm. Within two hours the main German trench line had been captured as well as the fearsome strongpoint named the 'Quadrilateral', to the east of the village, which had so dominated the ground between the village and Leuze Wood. The Irish regiments of the 16th Division once again were at the core of the fighting, but they had difficulty telling where exactly they were, as the now-flattened battlefield bore no identifiable landmarks: 'The village of Ginchy looked like a map of the pitted moon. Judgement of time and distance was submerged. Reeking fogs of high explosive hung in the air . . . always there were men seated in fantastic attitudes, silent with set, absorbed faces, busily engaged in trying to tie up staunch or plug their own wounds – to save their own single lives with their own hands.' The Guards Division came up and took over the smoking remains of the village and were watched in awe by Lance Corporal L. Lovell, of the Yorkshire Regiment: 'We were scruffy, unshaven and dirty and there they were, all clean and tidy, even their brasses were bright. We didn't know how they did it. What discipline, it was marvellous.'

Although Ginchy had fallen, the same fate had yet to await the stumps, shattered trees and waterlogged shell holes that were the stinking remains of High Wood, where III Corps had failed to take any ground, despite another mine having been detonated. The 1st Canadian Division had better fortune, for they advanced over 500 yards (457m) towards Martinpuich, and finally managed to connect with units of the 15th Division. From 10 to 14 September, most of the fighting fell to XIV Corps, which also had to ward off some strong counter-attacks in and around Ginchy. The Guards, meanwhile, advanced into the German trenches south-east of the Quadrilateral. At the far left of the line, II Corps were able to secure German trenches near Thiepval called the 'Wonder Work'. Few men realized the following day they were to witness an event that was to be unique in military history.

15–22 September: The Battle of Flers–Courcelette

The story of the development of the tank is too convoluted to be repeated in detail here. Suffice to say that like many innovations, the concept of an armoured fighting vehicle was not new, having been outlined by Renaissance artist Leonardo Da Vinci, among others. The tanks destined for use on the

Detail of the Battle of Flers–Courcelette 15–22 September.

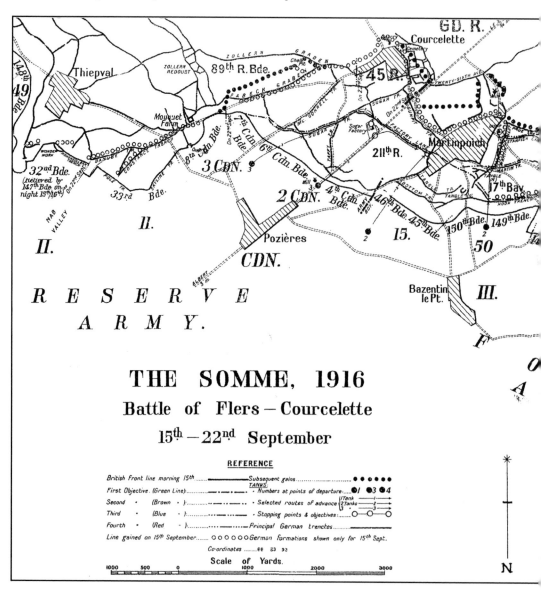

THE SOMME, 1916

Battle of Flers – Courcelette

15th – 22nd September

REFERENCE

British Front line morning 15th .... Subsequent gains .... ● ● ● ● ●
TANKS.
First Objective (Green Line)............ · Numbers at points of departure:....●1 ●3 ●4
Second   ·   (Brown ·).............. · Selected routes of advance {1Tank ——1——
{2Tanks ——2——
Third   ·   (Blue ·)............... · Stopping points & objectives:......O—O—O
Fourth   ·   (Red ·)............... Principal German trenches........
Line gained on 15th September....... O O O O O O German formations shown only for 15th Sept.
Co-ordinates 88 83 93
Scale of Yards.
1000   500   0   1000   2000   3000

N

Somme had been developed around an idea put forward by an officer in the Royal Engineers named Major Charles Swinton, which found favour with Winston Churchill, then First Lord of the Admiralty, who was publicly critical on the wisdom of sending 'brave men to chew on barbed wire'. He was angered at the failure of any of the senior generals to wage war at anything other than a traditional level, and he believed the stalemate on the Western Front could be broken only by embracing new ideas and concepts. The tank caught his imagination and he became one of its strongest supporters. The

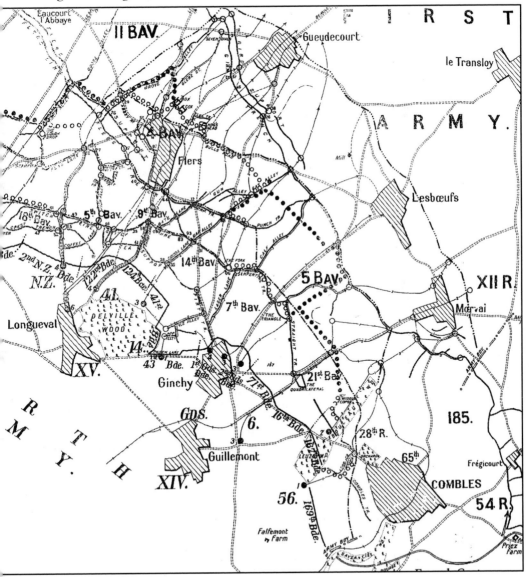

An original drawing of Sir John Dashwood's tank, C13 in Angle Wood valley. This MkI Tank has its steering wheels visible at the rear, which were designed to aid steering, but they proved largely useless and were subsequently removed from all vehicles (David Cohen Fine Art collection).

final design was left to two engineers named Tritton and Wilson, who devised a trapezoid with tracks that ran around the exterior of the body. All they had to do was develop it into a practical vehicle. It was first demonstrated to senior officers and selected politicians in January 1916, but despite grudging acceptance by the army, there was much political infighting in the War Office over how best to use the new weapons, and under whose command they should be placed. The Admiralty staked a claim to them, and insisted that as they mounted naval 6-pounder guns, they be referred to as 'Landships'. Haig, still faced with the demanding requirements of the Somme campaign, insisted that regardless of whom was to command them, they be put into action as soon as possible.

The men to crew these vehicles were drawn from every branch of the Armed Forces, but particularly valued were those with mechanical or driving ability, as well as trained machine-gunners. The unit was to be known as The Heavy Section (or Heavy Branch) Motor Machine-gun Corps. No matter how keen the men were to go into action, the fact could not be ignored by GHQ that they were neither fully trained nor up to strength in terms of personnel or vehicles. In August 1916, 150 tanks had been shipped to France from Fosters of Lincoln, but many were in a poor mechanical state due to constant demands by the army for demonstrations to VIPs of their trench crossing and wire-flattening abilities: efforts that had sorely tried the already exhausted crews, as well as placing a heavy mechanical strain on the fragile vehicles. Neither men nor machines were in any state to be used in a major offensive, but despite persuasive arguments that the tanks remain a closely guarded secret until 1917 – when some 500 would be available – Haig was undeterred in his determination to use them with all possible haste. Whether this was a wise decision is open to question, for there were too few to have any real effect on the course of the battle, and once used, the vital element of surprise would be lost. Nevertheless, Haig was for trying anything that might help in breaking the growing stalemate along the Somme. While his decision to commit so few vehicles across such a long battlefront has long been criticized, it must be appreciated that using them was still something of a leap of faith on his part, for they were a completely untested form of battle technology. Heedless of the controversy that raged around them, the men of the HBMMG moved up to their rallying points on 14 and 15 September. But at this eleventh hour a mere forty-nine vehicles were ready for combat. They were sparingly allocated to the Fourth Army as follows:

XIV Corps–C Company, seventeen tanks
XV Corps–D Company, seventeen tanks
III Corps–De Company, one section, eight tanks
Reserve Army–C Company, one section, seven tanks
GHQ Reserve–ten tanks, none serviceable

In reality, the situation was more dire than anyone had expected, for after a series of disastrous mechanical failures, as well as several vehicles ditching, only thirty-two tanks arrived at their starting points in time for Zero Hour. The frontage of the attack was to extend from Combles to Martinpuich, the intention being to breakthrough in the region of Morval–Gueudecourt–Flers. The vehicles would advance behind a creeping barrage in sections of two or three, their task being to flatten wire and destroy strongpoints, paying particular attention to machine-gun nests. At the far west of the line of attack, alongside Mouquet Farm, the Canadian Corps, comprising the 2nd and 3rd Divisions, were protecting the flank and their advance took the strong German trench line of Fabeck Graben that ran between the farm and Courcelette village. They had six tanks of No. 1 Section, C Company with them, but across the rough terrain the troops were able to advance faster than the tanks, leaving them behind to negotiate the shell-pocked ground. The 20th and 21st Infantry Battalions captured and cleared the dugouts under the old sugar factory with tank support from Captain Inglis in a machine named 'Crème de Menthe' of C Company. The Germans, already shell-shocked and exhausted, could not believe what they were seeing. One ran past his comrades shouting: 'There is

A study in enemies. The original picture, simply annotated on the back 'der Somme, 1916' shows a group of hardbitten German officers, NCOs and infantrymen. All the senior ranks carry holstered Luger pistols on their belts and two of the men wear the second-class Iron Cross. Most of these men were veterans of the battles of 1914 and 1915 and the loss of such experienced soldiers on the Somme was something the army could ill-afford (Author's collection).

a crocodile crawling into our lines!' When the Germans surrendered, one officer, upon seeing the tank, said: 'This is not war, but bloody butchery.' One cannot help but wonder what the Canadians, who had been on the receiving end of the first gas attack in April 1915 thought of this comment. Having secured the ground, they were forced to sit tight as a German bombardment pounded the line. They remained in place, however, and to their right the other brigades of III Corps launched their advance behind a heavy British barrage, with eight tanks accompanying the troops.

The task of the 15th (Scottish) Division was seemingly straightforward: to secure Martinpuich. Unfortunately, one of the accompanying tanks was hit and disabled by a shell before Zero Hour, but the other, numbered D20, commanded by Lieutenant Drader, advanced with the Scotsmen at dawn, and at once helped silence several machine-gun posts. Shortage of fuel forced Drader to retire about 7.30am, although it mattered little, for when the barrage lifted at 9.20am the infantry had entered the village and were ejecting the remaining Germans from their dugouts. By midafternoon, the 6th Cameronians managed to take the northern end of Martinpuich and were able to join with the flank of the Canadian Division. Of the other two divisions of III Corps, the 50th (Northumbrian) and 47th (2nd London), it was the 50th that had a marginally easier task, as they were to advance across open land to the east of Martinpuich, which was far easier terrain for the tanks to work along. One problem, however, was the division's frontage, which projected into the German lines and the attackers were exposed to flanking fire from both High Wood and Martinpuich. Tanks D24 and D25, commanded respectively by Lieutenants Stone and Colle, were parked less than 400 yards (365.7m) from the German trenches and at 5.47am, thirty-three minutes before Zero, they moved forward, the intention being to reach the enemy line five minutes before the infantry. But despite trying to mask their exhausts with wet sandbags, the clattering sound of their approach attracted immediate shellfire and D24 was hit, immobilizing it. D25 continued, moving along the eastern edge of Martinpuich and clearing out the strongpoints, much to the delight of the men of the 150th Brigade, who were following. Within an hour, the first objective had fallen and by 10.00am the second and third objectives had also been taken: but heavy shellfire forced some of these trenches to be abandoned. It was to take several more days for the scattered outposts to be linked and the line consolidated. Meanwhile, the 47th Division had drawn the short straw, and was sent into the horror that had become High Wood. If this was bad news for the infantry, it was doubly so for the four tank crews, who were accompanying them in vehicles D13, D21, D22, and C23. While tanks could negotiate shell holes, deep trenches, and even cross fallen trees, they were rendered helpless in High Wood's natural tank-traps: the dozens of shattered tree stumps that littered the ground. Their commanders could only hope there was sufficient open ground to enable them to advance, and D21 and D22 began their crawl forward twenty-nine minutes before Zero. Tanks D13 (commanded by Lieutenant Sampson and inevitably dubbed 'Delilah') and C23 had orders to follow separate routes, but all were to meet at the German front line half an hour later, which was a tall order considering the nature of the ground, which was a mass of tangled wire, shattered trees and shell holes. D22 emerged from the wood and promptly attacked the first trench it found, which unfortunately happened to be occupied by the 6th City of London Rifles. Mercifully, it became stuck fast before it did any serious damage. As the infantry began their assault on the wood, they met with devastating machine-gun fire and only after a tremendous effort by the 1/8th, 1/19th and the 1/20th Battalions of the London Regiment was the first line taken.

Campaign Chronicle

Meanwhile, two more tanks were in trouble. D13 – 'Delilah' – had had such a struggle over obstacles that at one point a heavy sponson door fell off, one crew member bravely jumping out and manhandling it back onto its hinges under enemy gunfire. The rough ground placed such a strain on the engine it eventually expired, leaving the tank a sitting duck for artillery, so the crew sensibly abandoned it. The infantry were making good progress, however, helped by a hurricane bombardment of 750 Stokes mortar shells that accurately pounded the German lines. The 1/21st and 1/24th Londons progressed up the western edge of the High Wood and dug in. Meanwhile, tank D21 had also entered the wood but travelled less than 50 yards (45.7m) before becoming hopelessly ditched in a British trench, shearing its rear axle in the process. On the division's left, the remaining vehicle was supporting the 17th Poplar and Stepney Rifles and the 18th London Irish Rifles, which was suffering from heavy enfilade fire. By then C23 was irretrievably stuck in No Man's Land, though it tried to use its 6-pounder guns to help the attacking infantry, but to no great effect. The survivors of the division dug in along a series of posts and switch trenches on a front that now had no discernible line. Private Eccles of the Rifle Brigade was forced to walk across a carpet of dead Germans lying on the bottom of their newly captured trench. He froze, and his sergeant demanded

This photo shows a happy group men from the 51st Highland Division. Not for nothing did the Germans refer to these kilted soldiers as 'Ladies from Hell'. The sight of these faces behind a rifle and bayonet would be enough to make the most stout-hearted soldier quail (Royal Armouries).

The Tank

There were two variants of tank: 'male' and 'female'. A 'male' was armed with two 6-pounder guns and two machine-guns, was designed to deal with gun emplacements and fortified strongpoints, and was recognizable by its much larger sponsons. The early 'females' had four Vickers machine-guns and were to be used primarily against enemy infantry and machine-guns. Each tank carried a crew of eight: a commander, driver, four gunners and two gearsmen. The vehicles were powered by a six-cylinder 105hp Daimler engine, and weighed 28 tons (28.4 tonnes), having a maximum speed of 3.7mph on level ground. Forty-six gallons (209 litres) of high-octane aviation petrol was carried in the front 'horns', giving a maximum fighting range of 23 miles (37km). The temperature in the cramped interior was normally over 100 degrees Celsius, and the cabin was filled with exhaust, cordite, and petrol fumes that were highly toxic. After combat, crews normally needed twenty-four hours of rest to recover.

---

to know why: 'I don't like treading on their faces,' he said plaintively. 'Never mind the bloody faces, MOVE!' Eccles waded through the remains, fighting the urge to vomit.

The cost in casualties was high – thousands – and in the III Corps area the tanks had largely been wasted, due to the actions of the corps commander, General Pulteney, who ignored the advice of other officers to allow the tanks to skirt the woods, and insisted on sending them straight into it. In the end, it was the infantry flanking attacks that were to secure High Wood, but at a terrible cost. The battalions of the 141st Brigade were sorely reduced after the battle, having virtually no officers left to command them. And yet the division finally captured its objective: two months to the day from its first attack, when High Wood had been there for the taking.

The brightest part of the battle was the success of the 41st Division and its capture of Flers. Attached to XV Corps, the ten tanks of D Company went into action at first light. Two immediately became 'bellied' in the soft ground, their weight pressing their steel underbellies up on the exposed flywheels of the engine, stalling it. Their commanders, Lieutenants Cort and Huffam, could only stand on their tanks' roofs and watch the remaining five vehicles heading towards the opening barrage on the German lines. Huffam recalled: 'It was a wonderful experience. A barrage of terrific intensity; the rising ground in front seemed to disappear. Jerry took one look at our tanks rolling towards him, rose from his trenches in front of Flers and fled back into the village.' Ironically, in the afternoon, when Cort and Huffam's two tanks were recovered, they proved to be the only serviceable vehicles available. Both headed into Flers, and Huffam had his first taste of combat. His driver was soon blinded by metal splinters and Huffam pulled him aside, taking control of the vehicle. As they followed Cort's tank, it received a direct hit from a shell. Seconds later, his own tank, 'Dolly', also received a direct hit, Huffam coming-to outside the wreck, lying on top of the dead body of his corporal, Sanders. The blast relieved Huffam of his teeth, hair and memory, but he was alive at least, unlike the remainder of the two crews.

The other tanks were suffering mixed fortunes through breakdowns and damage inflicted by shellfire, and it was left to vehicle D17, commanded by Lieutenant S.H. Hastie, to make military history by capturing the village of Flers. Hastie, whose Scottish ancestry was recorded in the tank's name, 'Dinnaken', was steering the vehicle doggedly towards the village in an attempt to assist the hard-pressed infantry of the 122nd and 123rd Brigades, suffering casualties from the inevitable machine-gunfire. As 'Dinnaken' rumbled through the streets, Lieutenant Phillips, an RFC observer of No. 3 Squadron, flying overhead, relayed a message to GHQ, which was subsequently widely misreported in the Press as: 'A tank is walking up the high street of Flers with the British Army cheering behind.' In fact, the mixed London units of the brigade were doing anything but cheering as they dealt with fierce opposition from Germans in the ruined houses and cellars, who were pouring intense gunfire and grenade bombardment onto D17, as well as three other tanks that were working their way along the edge of the village. For many British soldiers, of course, the sight of the tanks was as bewildering as it was to the Germans. A few had heard rumours of a secret British weapon, but then rumours were never scarce. To those who saw a tank for the first time, the experience was to be indelibly imprinted on their minds. Private C.J. Arthur later recorded his thoughts as the division attacked:

'The tanks were at once a delight and disappointment. They were easily ditched, but at the same time they were impregnable. I saw a party of the enemy clamber onto one . . . after firing at it at point-blank with a machine-gun and throwing bombs from 5 yards [4.5m]. I saw another [tank] run along a thick belt of wire . . . and so clear the way for us. Yet another spotted a machine-gun in a house in Flers; the fellow wandered up the road, did a sharp turn and ambled through the house.'

Despite the best efforts of the tanks, the New Zealanders of the 2nd NZ Brigade

Soldiers cluster around Tank D17 at Flers, broken down and being used as an impromptu brigade HQ. Their novelty value made them irresistible to passing troops and crews who were forced to leave them made sure they were firmly padlocked. The complex camouflage scheme proved pointless as mud quickly coated the vehicles (Tank Museum, Bovington).

were doubly unlucky as they advanced from north-west of Longueval, for they were not only enfiladed by machine-guns situated in High Wood but also caught in the ensuing British barrage. Nevertheless, by 8.30am they had captured the support trenches in front of Flers. There they stopped, held up by wire, which tanks D11 and D12 obligingly crushed for them. The troops eventually managed to dig in and consolidate as the Bavarian units holding the lines retreated towards Gueudecourt.

For the infantry of XIV Corps, who were fighting their way between Flers and Combles, the tanks proved of little help, indeed one tank officer was told in no uncertain terms by an infantry officer to: 'Take your damn stink-box away' as it was attracting unwelcome levels of shellfire. The Guards Division was to have had assistance from ten tanks, but five failed to reach the starting point and the five surviving tanks were not to be of great use to them. On the Guards' right flank one broke down, while another became hopelessly lost. On the left flank, two more tanks got lost, while one bogged down in the mud. The remaining tank, a 'male', numbered 760, commanded by Lieutenant Elliott, ran low on petrol and was forced to turn back. Despite these setbacks, the Guards performed well, and by 11.15am had captured their initial objectives beyond Ginchy. The 6th Division, slightly south of the Guards, had advanced at 6.20am towards the Quadrilateral Redoubt, just east of the village, and were to have been aided by three tanks. But only one, C22, commanded by Lieutenant B. Henriques, was in a fit state to join the battle. It advanced under a hail of machine-gunfire that was so heavy it shattered the periscopes and driving prisms and turned the boiler plate red-hot with bullet impacts. Armour piercing bullets also made life trying, punching through the plate and injuring all the crew to such an extent that it was forced to retire: proving that despite outward appearances, the tanks were not impregnable. This was unfortunate for the advancing regiments, for the 1st Leicestershire and 9th Norfolks had moved through the Quadrilateral but were stopped by uncut wire the tank could have made short work of. They were then driven back by fire from the defending 21st (1st Pomeranian) Infantry.

Meanwhile, by 6.20am, on the right flank of the battle area, the Territorials of the 56th (London) Division were on their way into No Man's Land from their jumping off trenches between Leuze Wood and Combles. Fortunately for them, they were to have tank support that was to prove effective. Three tanks, C13, C14, and C16, were allocated and they had left their starting point at 8pm on the night of 14th to ensure they arrived in good time for Zero Hour. C16, commanded by Lieutenant E. Purdey, accompanied the 1/2nd, 1/5th, 1/9th and 1/16th Londons in their advance on Combles village and a heavily defended strongpoint called

'The Loop'. Combles was a difficult objective. It lay in a valley and was therefore invisible to British artillery observers, thus escaping bombardment. Left to their own devices, the Germans had spent months reinforcing its cellars and machine-gun posts, turning it into a small fortress. Unfortunately, a British shell fell short and blew off the left track of C16, leaving it stranded, but not helpless, for the crew turned it into a steel pillbox, using its four Vickers guns against the Germans with devastating effect: a fusillade they kept up for some five hours. The War Diary of the 1/2nd London Regiment recorded dryly that 'the tank's material effect against hostile troops was considerable.' Despite this assistance, the brigade infantry failed to reach their objective and had to dig in 80 yards (73m) short. The Royal Fusiliers and Middlesex Regiments of 167th Brigade advanced through Leuze Wood on the heels of C14, commanded by Lieutenant Arnold, whose appearance in front of the German 28th Reserve Infantry Regiment led to men rubbing their eyes in disbelief. Lieutenant Noajk, a company commander, said later of the event that he initially thought the tank was some sort of giant farm threshing machine, though he rapidly changed his mind when its machine-guns opened fire on his trench. With the tank assistance, the infantry reached their objective and C14 continued on its merry way, heading towards Bouleux Wood. But the infantry following were stopped by accurate gunfire from the wood and forced to pull back, so it was not until early evening the ground was taken by the 1/1st London and 1/7th Middlesex.

Along the front, the Germans had been driven back about 2,500 yards (2.2km) – over 3,500 yards (3.2km) around Flers itself – and in relative terms, this was bordering on a wholesale advance. As far as the tanks were concerned, while many were undoubtedly uselessly squandered, their crews learned valuable lessons about trench fighting and the abilities (or lack thereof) of their machines when used in difficult or unsuitable terrain. The tanks clearly needed to be provided with better armour, more powerful engines, and to be used more efficiently in a tactical sense, if they were to work effectively with the infantry. Meanwhile, GHQ remained, for the most part, unimpressed with the performance of the new weapon, General Fielding reporting to Rawlinson on 19 September that: 'they were of no assistance in the attack, chiefly owing to the fact that they started too late . . . and also owing to the fact that the moment they started they lost all sense of direction and wandered about aimlessly.' This was an unfair assessment in view of the lack of preparation time given to the tank crews, the limited visibility they had in combat, and the fact that even seasoned infantry officers became disorientated in the featureless terrain.

In the days following the Flers–Courcelette attack, much time was to be spent by the infantry in reinforcing and consolidating, although all three corps

Troops move over the featureless landscape during the attack on Ginchy, September 1916. The ground is mercifully dry at this point, but was not to remain so for long. The lack of identifiable features in the surrounding landscape gives some idea of the difficulty in finding objectives during an attack (R. Dunning).

were to continue fighting in some small pockets. In particular, III Corps' 3rd Canadian Division managed to enter the outskirts of what was left of the strongpoint at Mouquet Farm, while the rest of the divisions (the 15th, 50th and 47th) took part in limited objective attacks that mostly proved abortive. On XV Corps' front, the story was similar, with a tank-supported attack by the 41st Division being repulsed, and the 20th New Zealanders launching an abortive attack. The 14th Division had tried to advance east and west of the Ginchy–Gueudecourt road but without success. Even the Guards of XIV Corps were suffering, the 2nd Brigade having finally captured a section of the Ginchy–Lesboeufs road (their third objective on the morning of 16th) only to spend the rest of the day fending off German counter-attacks. Meanwhile, the

3rd Guards Brigade advance was stopped by intense machine-gunfire, obliging troops to dig in with heavy losses. The greatest success on 18 September was the final capture of the Quadrilateral Redoubt by troops of the 6th Division.

26 September: The Further Battle for Thiepval Ridge

On the Reserve Army's front — the original Somme battlefront — the fight to secure Thiepval Ridge was on once again, under the aegis of II Corps and its attached Canadian Division. If the line south of the ridge was to be taken and held, then Thiepval had to fall. It dominated the ground around it and the longer it was in German hands, the stronger it became. By September, along every few yards of the front there was a reinforced German dugout, cellar or firing point. The enemy clung tenaciously to the ridge, knowing that its loss would seriously compromise their ability to maintain their line. At the extreme left of the line, the 18th Division's 53rd and 54th Brigades assaulted the pulverized remains of the village, with the 54th at the extreme left. The 11th Royal Fusiliers entered the German front line, bombing and shooting their way along, in company with the 12th Middlesex Regiment. The men had learned a great deal about fighting in the rubble and cellars and they nominated mopping up parties of grenade men. Germans who refused to surrender were bombed-out and others who emerged expecting to fire on the backs of the passing British found themselves facing tough, well-armed men. Rarely was any quarter asked for or given, and the fighting was bitter but successful. By midafternoon Thiepval village — or what little dust remained of it — had fallen to the British. Next to the village, the 53rd Brigade had sensibly been ordered to take up positions well in front of the British line. This saved many casualties when the alert German artillery suddenly unleashed a hurricane bombardment on the lines: it took the 8th Suffolks and 8th Norfolks less than fifteen minutes to reach, and then overwhelm, the German lines. They were helped by two tanks, one of which was quickly ditched. The other made it into Schwaben Trench, where it became stuck, the crew being forced to abandon it. Further attempts to get beyond the trenches running behind the village were stopped by heavy fire and the Suffolks were forced to dig in. Meanwhile, the 33rd and 34th Brigades of 11th Division had to take the ground dominated by Mouquet Farm. It would not be an easy task. The battalions of the 33rd still had strongly fortified German trenches in front of them, but were able to use the hundreds of overlapping shell holes to find some protection from the machine-gunfire. The 6th Border Regiment and 9th Sherwood Foresters made good progress, and by dusk had made a comprehensive job of forcing the Germans out of their trenches.

To their right, the 34th Division, which had suffered so grievously on 1 July, had, after a conference of commanding officers, adopted slightly different tactics. Small parties of shock troops – mostly tough Lancashire Fusiliers, well supplied with grenades – had crept out before Zero Hour and blocked the entrances to the German dugouts around the strongpoints under Mouquet Farm. The 8th Northumberland Fusiliers and the 9th Lancashire Fusiliers rushed it, sustaining heavy casualties as they faced a withering hail of fire from German support trenches behind the farm. So accurate was the shooting that only one officer and about fifty men were able to take shelter in the trenches, and the battalion had to be relieved by the 11th Manchesters. The plan was for help to be provided by two tanks, both of which bogged down before they reached enemy lines. All was not lost though, for the infantry were assisted by the crew of one 'male' tank, appropriately named, 'We're All In It', who, using the tank for protection, dismounted their Lewis guns and opened fire on the assembled German troops. By 1.30pm all the objectives had been taken, including most of Hessian Trench, which ran the full-length of the ground behind Thiepval and Mouquet Farm. While the farm may have fallen, it was by no means an end to the struggle to prise the rest of the line from enemy hands.

On 26 September, between Thiepval and Courcelette, the Canadian Corps moved up toward Stuff and Regina Trenches, which ran along the higher ground behind the two villages. The 1st Canadian Division managed to cross No Man's Land unscathed, in the main, but the 15th (48th Highland) Battalion lagged behind and left their flank dangerously open, permitting enfilade fire to cause losses. Undeterred, they kept up their momentum and entered the German lines. Corporal Bennett of the 90th Rifles later wrote:

'We got into the Huns' lines and had a real stiff fight with bombs and

---

The Hand Grenade

By 1916 the hand grenade had become the primary weapon for trench warfare. The weapon had two types. The German stick, or 'potato masher' grenade was a defensive pattern, with fairly large explosive charge in its thin steel body. It was very effective in confined spaces where the blast effect was magnified but it had little fragmentation capability. The British Mills bomb, adopted in April 1915 was the most prolific Allied type and was an offensive grenade, designed to shatter into lethal fragments that would spread out for about 30 feet (9.1m). Some 60 million Mills grenades were manufactured during the war.

No one was immune from the weather and a French soldier attempts, probably for the benefit of the camera, to empty some liquid mud from his trench. Such effort was largely a waste of time and effort. Worth noting is the huge roll of barbed wire on the fire-step, probably awaiting laying out in No Man's Land (Jacques Moreau photo).

bayonets. They (the Germans) were popping up from trenches and dugouts and sometime they were in front of us, sometimes behind. I picked up a German automatic pistol and used it as it was much better for close fighting than my rifle. I kept that gun and it came in real useful in later fighting.'

The 2nd Division attacked the defences behind Courcelette and had two tanks in support, both of which were soon knocked out of action. Despite taking many casualties, a company of the 27th (City of Winnipeg) Infantry reached their objective, where they dug in and fought off two heavy counter-attacks. All the attacking units, in particular the 31st Battalion, took heavy casualties because of accurate shelling, but by midmorning enough men had entered the trenches to force the 72nd (4th Thuringian Infantry) Regiment back and establish a line of interconnected outposts. East of Martinpuich, the 50th Division of III Corps had attacked but achieved little, except to add to the growing casualty roll. It was eighty-three days since the first Somme attacks had been launched, and at last it was becoming clear to British observers that German resistance was weakening across the front, and in places units were retreating, although the exact reason was still unknown.

25–28 September: The Battle of Morval

GHQ wanted to capitalize on the success of Flers–Courcelette and maintain the impetus of the advance, so with the French at the southern extreme of the battlefield they decided to launch another major assault at midday of the 21st. Nature had other plans though, for the relatively dry weather had broken and it rained solidly, slowing troop movement and supply convoys. After a few days' inactivity the 25th was deemed the most suitable date to resume the attacks along a front extending from beyond Flers to Gueudecourt and running south to Lesboeufs, pushing the line forward into a gentle curve running from Martinpuich, west of Combles, just above the River Somme. There was to be limited tank assistance, most of the vehicles by this time being under repair after their previous efforts, but at last the Fourth Army was beginning to understand the lessons of the previous months. Staff planning was improving, as was artillery coordination, resulting in the improved efficiency of creeping barrages: now a potent weapon of assault. At 12.35pm the attack began with a powerful artillery barrage along the whole front. Behind it, the corps of the Fourth Army advanced once more, with every expectation of success. The III Corps, just to the front and east of Martinpuich, moved forward with two tanks, the sight of which brought down a fierce German barrage on the unfortunate men of 68th Brigade, who were mainly Northumberland Fusiliers, effectively stopping the attack in its tracks. The XV Corps had slightly better luck, for its objective was the heavily defended Gird Trench and the village of Gueudecourt. The 21st Division advanced and partly captured its objective, but was then halted by thick wire and machine-gunfire. A single 'female' tank,

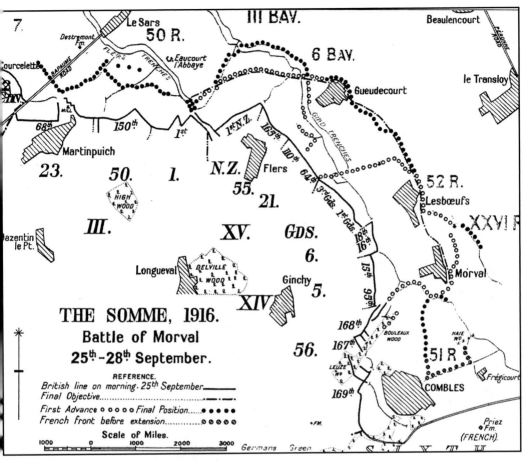

The Battle of Morval 25–28 September.

commanded by 2nd Lieutenant C. Storey, was summoned and went into attack at dawn on the morning of the 26th, driving the Germans from their trenches and flattening the wire. As the tank lumbered into view, the Germans promptly surrendered to it, so that in under an hour, some 1,500 yards (1.3km) of trench, fourteen machine-guns, 362 German soldiers, and eight officers had been captured, for the loss of only five British soldiers. As the report of XV Corps commander, Lieutenant General H.S. Horne, later states: 'What would have proved a very difficult operation, involving probably heavy losses, was taken with the greatest ease entirely owing to the assistance rendered by the tank.' It was a fine example of tank and infantry coordination. The cavalry was sent to reconnoitre, finding the village largely abandoned. By midafternoon it had been occupied.

Shrapnel Helmets

The steel helmet was a comparatively late addition to the infantryman's equipment. The French Adrian helmet was adopted in 1915, but it was thin and provided minimal protection. German soldiers wore the spiked leather *Pickelhaube* until early 1915 when the distinctive *Stalhelm* began to be issued. The British 'Brodie' helmet was not issued until early 1916, and so few were available that battalions in the front line had to hand them over to their replacements. It is estimated that shrapnel helmets prevented about 80 per cent of fatal head wounds. By the time of the Somme battles soldiers on both sides wore the 'tin hat', and it has since become a potent symbol of modern warfare.

The 55th Division had managed by sheer determination to get some of its troops into a sunken road between Gird Trench and Gueudecourt, where they hung on desperately. Corporal A.N. Parry of the 1/6th King's Regiment was amid the fighting:

'We got some shelter from the machine-guns in the sunken road, which the Germans occupied. It wasn't a road really, but a wide trench with dugouts and wire. Our shells had smashed it up and there were dead Germans and bits of Germans everywhere. We used them as sandbags to shelter behind and I got my Lewis (gun) going. My No. 2 was shot dead right next to me and I got a tremendous whack on my tin hat, I don't know from what but it near knocked me senseless. I was dizzy but helped fight off a counter-attack and that Lewis was worth a company of men. Eventually things got quieter and I got taken back to a dressing station to have my head looked at as I was bleeding heavily. I didn't care what happened after that.'

25–28 September: The Battle of Morval

What actually happened was the New Zealand Division formed a link between III Corps on their left, and XV Corps on their right, in the newly won ground north of Flers, and dig in.

The XIV Corps, north and east of Ginchy, had a hard task in capturing both Lesboeufs and Morval to their front. The infantry brigades of the 5th Division were facing Morval and it was the 1st Devons who managed to enter the German trenches and bomb their way down them until they took the strongpoint that lay across the Ginchy–Morval road. The 2nd Grenadier Guards were stopped by wire, which astonishingly in the face of so much hostile fire, they managed to cut and they then proved unstoppable, storming the trenches in front of them. The 1st Cheshires and 2nd King's Own Scottish Borderers captured and held the northern and southern outskirts of Morval, the village being in British hands by early afternoon. At the same time,

A poignant image of Australians heading towards Poziers. How many glancing up at the camera would survive the fighting? Their varied headgear and casual appearance were typical of ANZAC soldiers, whose often unsoldierly appearance belied their tremendous fighting spirit (Australian War Memorial).

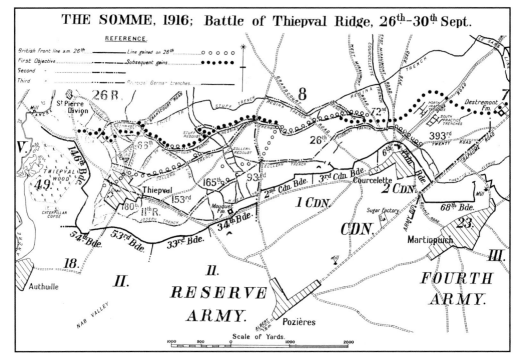

The Reserve Army attack on Thiepval Ridge, 26–30 September 1916.

battalions of the 6th Division were attacking the Morval–Lesboeufs road, which they also captured, thus forming a link with the Guards Brigade to their left. It was left to the 56th Division (London) Territorials to take the heavily defended set of trenches from the 56th (7th Westphalia) Infantry around Bouleux Wood, north of Combles, which by lunchtime they had done: capturing eighty prisoners and four machine-guns into the bargain. The London Scottish gained special praise for performing effectively in the attack, by taking a vital section of trench that overlooked the Combles–Morval Valley, which finally provided the attacking troops with the advantage of high ground.

The following morning, the 27 September, was to see no let-up in the impetus of the fighting, as British troops struggled to consolidate positions and link with their flanking units. It was once again the turn of the Commonwealth troops – Canadians and New Zealanders – to help with the attack, and both divisions were to be in the toughest part of the fighting. The most difficult task was in ensuring captured trenches could withstand increasingly desperate German counter-attacks, although admittedly these were proving to be weaker than previously experienced, as German infantry units gradually withdrew. Despite this, the Allied troops had to move forward over hotly contested ground: a slow business that could only be done shell hole by shell hole and trench by trench. The fighting was taking place in increasingly abysmal weather, as heavy rain set in, and while it was still relatively mild, the pervasive mud did nothing to lighten the spirits of the exhausted men.

The various army corps still engaged in the battle were having mixed fortunes as the initial impetus of their attack diminished. From Thiepval the line now ran due east past Courcelette and Martinpuich to Flers, then curved south to Morval and Combles, where the French Sixth Army was holding the flank. At Thiepval Ridge the 55th Brigade of the 18th Division was trying to consolidate the Zollern Trench system and rid it of remaining pockets of resistance. But the fighting was hard. It took a surprise barrage of Stokes mortars at 6.30am and the combined weight of three infantry battalions – the 5th Dorsets and 11th Manchesters reinforced by the 9th West Yorks – to advance and capture a mere 50 yards (45.7m) of trench, which was not cleared until 9pm. To their right, the 7th South Staffords and the 9th Border Regiment managed to get far enough ahead to take the remaining trenches of Stuff Redoubt, but the following morning they were heavily attacked by Germans still occupying parts of the infamous Schwaben Redoubt. Only vicious hand-to-hand fighting retrieved the situation, but the brigade troops were spent, and unable to maintain further progress.

On the morning of the 27th, the troops of II Corps' 33rd and 34th Brigades were astonished to find the Germans had evacuated the Zollern Redoubt. Units of the 11th Manchesters, 5th Dorsets and 9th Lancashire Fusiliers immediately moved into the empty trenches. As darkness fell, it was decided the Manchesters would make a night attack, and despite the disadvantages of fighting in the rain and mud – and by the glare of Very lights – they managed to advance successfully on their right. The fighting continued throughout the following day and it was not until 4pm on the 30th that men of the 7th South Staffordshire Regiment managed to push back the enemy on their flank and contact the neighbouring Canadians.

The 1st and 2nd Canadian Divisions, meanwhile, had been in the thick of things on a broad front of over 3,000 yards (2.7km) that curved round behind the village of Courcelette. It was vital they maintained contact with the troops of the Fourth Army's III Corps on their right, for any gap would be instantly exploited by the Germans. Under cover of intense shellfire, patrols found the Germans opposite were withdrawing and some Canadian Infantry battalions, including the 29th Vancouver, 31st Alberta and 28th North West, began to creep forward. But the enemy machine-gunners on their left flank were wide awake and their Maxims repulsed all attempts by the Canadians to advance. At

Campaign Chronicle

dawn on the 28th an assault was launched to try to eject the Germans from the maze of trenches behind Courcelette, but in attacks staged midafternoon, then again at 8.30pm, three successive waves of troops were defeated by intense gunfire. Almost without exception the men were driven back to their starting point. A Canadian sapper, Corporal E. Rossiter, MM, had the unenviable job of laying phone wires as the attack moved forward: 'We tried to keep in the communication trench as far as we could go, but it was so blown in by shellfire that we had to get out into the open. Imagine laying those goddam wires in the daylight diving from shell hole to shell hole. We made a dash and jumped into one . . . and there were five Canadians lying dead there. Jesus! It gave me a fright.' Fighting for the ground ebbed and flowed, with the Germans and Canadians constantly attacking and counter-attacking the same positions. By the final day of September, the lines had mostly stagnated in front of strong defensive works known as Regina and Stuff Trenches, which defeated all attempts at storming them.

For the New Zealanders, some gains had been made as they pushed forward from their trenches behind Flers, and they were able to secure the German trenches on their right, but Maxims sited between Eaucourt l'Abbaye and Gueudecourt caught the advancing 1st Otago Battalion, which lost over 300 men, as they worked their way up the slope. The New Zealanders eventually dug in, forming a salient between their two objectives, which quickly became a focal point for German artillery. To their right, XV Corps made a dawn attack on Gird Trench that ran just south of Gueudecourt and Lesboeufs. While all the British attacks were invariably met with deadly machine-gun fire, it was not one-sided, and the Machine Gun Corps did sterling work for the attacking troops by laying down protective barrages and concentrating on counter-battery work. Not for nothing were the MGC known as 'The Suicide Squad', for their positions inevitably attracted concentrated fire from enemy artillery and snipers. Sergeant George Butler of the 12th Machine Gun Company was part of the relief force sent to Lesboeufs. The Germans were nowhere to be seen, though heavy shellfire fell constantly, and conditions were deteriorating rapidly in the rain:

'There was no shelter anywhere, only shell holes. It had taken a long time to get up to the line at Lesboeufs. We walked all the way, through thousands and thousands of shell holes, rim to rim. Every time you put a foot forward you sank, and you were sinking into a mass of dead as well as mud. We had nothing to eat for three days — no food! We lost three guns and more than a dozen men. Eventually my gun was the only one left. I decided that we'd fire all the ammunition we had off into No Man's

The badly wounded were taken by ambulance to hospitals behind the lines. The most hopeless cases were often left in special wards while the less seriously hurt were operated on. Those who proved hardy enough to still be alive the next day would be rapidly transferred to receive attention. Despite the incredible strain they were under, the medical services performed extraordinarily well during the Somme campaign (Author's collection).

At the southern edge of the Somme, soldiers of the French 7th Infantry wait listlessly during a pause from marching to the front line. The amount of equipment they carried was as prodigious as that of the British and can be seen from the size of their packs (Jacques Moreau photo).

Land – I was practically buried in empties when we'd finished. I said to my men "pick up your kit, we're off out." I knew I could be shot for it, but I couldn't see the sense of staying.'

On the night of the 27th, the Brigades of XIV Corps between Lesboeufs and Combles were relieved by French troops. On 30 September, the 23rd Division managed to take Destremont Farm, between Courcelette and Le Sars, which had been holding out despite fierce artillery bombardments and repeated attacks. At last this enabled the brigade to contact the Canadians on their left flank. Further along the line, the 47th Division, with some help from the New Zealanders, pushed the Germans back and dug in. Thus September drew to a muddy close.

1–31 October: The Battle of the Ancre Heights

To the far left of the line along the Thiepval Ridge, II Corps was still attempting to crush the Schwaben Redoubt. On the 4th a pincer attack was launched by battalions of the 18th Division, but the ground had become so bad the men literally stuck in their tracks. Some idea of how bad the conditions had become can be gained from an account given by a Guards Private, J.L. Bouch: 'We came to a sunken road, narrow and fairly steep at the sides . . . and we slithered to the bottom without any bother. Do you think we could get up? No matter how we clawed we just kept slipping back. You couldn't sit down, you just kept sinking in the mud.' Eventually the 39th Division relieved the exhausted 18th and the fresh troops redoubled their efforts to take the redoubt. On the night of 9 October the 16th Sherwood Foresters succeeded in taking most of it, only to be forced out by a determined counter-attack. Next to them the 25th Division finally entered Stuff Redoubt, and with the help of reinforcements, formed a bridgehead. They held it against repeated counter-attacks, including the use of flame-throwers. The 47th Division managed to push past the ruins of Eaucourt l'Abbaye but the fighting was to continue on and off for the next week, as II Corp's 18th, 25th and 39th Divisions, and the Canadian 2nd Division, kept pushing at the Germans, who still occupied the now featureless wasteland of splintered trees, waterlogged shell holes, and ruinous trenches that had once been the Thiepval Ridge and forest. By that evening the 16th Sherwood Foresters had forced their way into the Schwaben and the 25th Division finally ejected the defenders of Stuff Redoubt. It was clear the Germans were making a planned withdrawal, yet it still took until 14 October for a few companies of 8th Loyal North Lancs to overrun the trenches north of the Schwaben, which provided them with a grandstand view of Grandcourt and enabled them to enfilade the rest of the Schwaben Redoubt. It was then left to the tired infantrymen of the 39th Division to make a final assault on it and it was carried predominantly by the men of the 4/5th Black Watch, who went over the parapet at 2.45pm and were still fighting hard at 11pm: by then reinforced by 1/1st Cambridge and the 17th Kings Royal Rifles. A private in the KRRC, A. Hales, said of the fight:

'They (the Germans) wouldn't give up, and we fought with bombs and
Lewis guns for every bay in every trench. We were helped by the fire from

As conditions deteriorated, it became more difficult to move around the battlefield. Here, a soldier leads a mule over a flooded duckboard track, and in the ceaseless rain of October and November even these soon floated away, leaving the ground virtually impassable (Author's collection).

our flank, particularly one Lewis gun that cut down any German who tried to get over the ground in front and we had a terrible time of it. Men were killed all around me and a stick bomb blew the head off the sergeant in front of me,

but I wasn't scratched. The Scotchmen were fighting mad and they Jerries eventually ran. I bloody would have done too, if they'd come at me.'

Despite several German counter-attacks, the men of the 39th Division hung on grimly and by 16 October the line was well enough established for them to be relieved by the 63rd Royal Naval Division. The whole northern sector above the Ancre river was now in British hands, and as far was possible, in the wet weather, the troops attempted to dig in. It took almost a week to consolidate their positions but finally, on 22 October, the 25th Division was relieved by the 19th Division, which took over the line east of Thiepval to the edge of the Poziers–Miramont road, linking with the flank of the 18th Division. It was not to be a time of rest though, for the Germans made a surprise counter-attack at dawn on 21 October, to pushing out the battalions lodging in the Schwaben Redoubt. The troops of 116th Brigade were thrown into the defence and with the assistance of its sister brigade, the 117th, recovered the position and even managed to advance as well. The entire corps was then sent into the attack, the 25th Division to the right, using two brigades to move towards Grandcourt, but the attack petered out when they ran into their own barrage, which caused heavy casualties and effectively broke up the attack. On their right flank, the 18th Division fared better, moving across the Flers–Courcelette road and entering the German trenches, where a standing fight erupted, lasting several hours. It was eventually decided in favour of the British by the timely arrival of

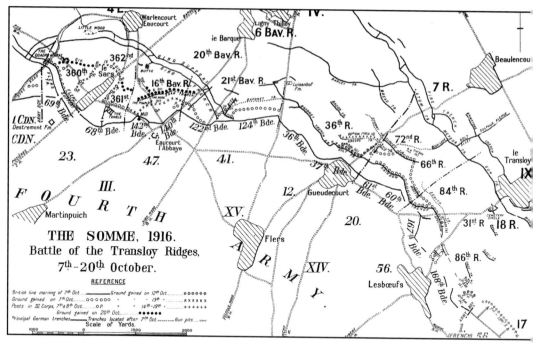

The Battle of the Transloy Ridges, 7–20 October 1916.

reinforcements in the form of the 11th Lancashire Fusiliers, whose presence — and endless supply of Mills grenades — forced the Germans to retire. North of Courcelette the Canadian 4th Corps, on the far right of the line, was ordered to attack at the odd time of 12.06pm, which they did, materially assisted by artillery and an effective overhead barrage from the Vickers guns of the Machine Gun Corps. As a result they were able to take their objectives with few casualties, pushing well beyond Destremont Farm, up to the lines south-east of Grandcourt, where they spent the rest of the day fighting off German counter-attacks. Further advances over the following four days were not so successful, being beaten off by artillery and machine-gun fire. As the temperature began to drop and the rain continued, the battle for the Ancre heights slowly petered out.

1–31 October: The Battle of Transloy Ridge

The last day of September saw the Allies, and Sir Douglas Haig in particular, in a hopeful frame of mind. The Morval battle had enabled a more or less continuous line to be established in what was once strongly held German

1–31 October: The Battle of Transloy Ridge

territory. But this was not the victory it appeared. While maintaining an effective rearguard action, the Germans had been frantically constructing three new trench lines along the Transloy Ridge, some 3 miles (4.8km) in depth. In effect, this meant any attacking troops would have to undergo yet another series of costly frontal attacks to reach open, undefended ground. No one in all honesty could claim the army was now up to the demands that such fighting would make. Casualties had been huge, with losses of over 400,000 British and Commonwealth troops, and reinforcements were physically soft, finding conditions particularly difficult. Nevertheless, Haig held his army in high regard, even if some of his senior officers questioned the ability of their brigades to continue to wage such a costly form of warfare against heavily defended objectives. Haig was determined to see his plan followed through to its conclusion and there was some sound logic to his thinking, for as the temperature continued to plummet and the rain fell unabated, it became obvious that it would not be long before conditions became impossible for fighting. The battle was again to be a series of small, set piece attacks, aimed at

Fourth Army area of operations, Le Sars to Le Transloy, 23 October–5 November 1916.

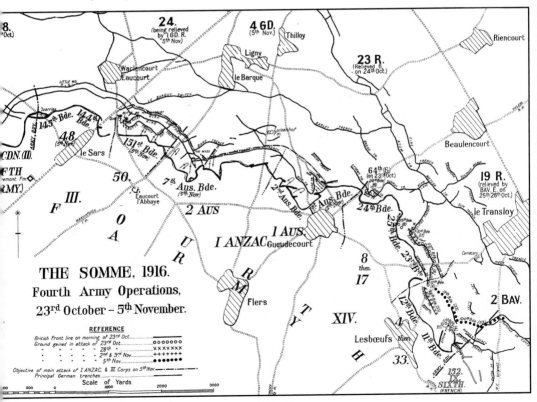

Campaign Chronicle

Manhandling an 18-pounder field gun out of the mud. The conditions here are not a bad as the later months of the Somme campaign, but the sheer effort involved is clear to see. By November some guns had sunk so deeply the crews were forced to abandon them. Many are presumably there to this day (Royal Armouries).

specific objectives. The strongly fortified Transloy Ridge was an escarpment that ran along the front of the village of the same name, and it ensured the British would once again be attacking up a slope. Tanks were called upon to help the attack forward and this time, given better ground to work along, they proved their worth. The first few days of the attack saw some important gains. At Le Sars, the Canadian 2nd Division, fighting with the 23rd Division, moved forward from its positions north of Courcelette and fierce fighting – involving bombs, bayonets and rifle butts – ensued, as the Germans fought desperately to recapture the lost ground. The Canadians moved through to the edge of Le Sars and on their right, III Corps' 47th Division managed to force its way into Eaucourt l'Abbaye, passing through it and finally overrunning the Flers Switch, which the German defenders had bravely held onto despite the mighty weight of shelling the British had pounded it with. Private G. McKenna of the 1/18th London Regiment (London Irish) saw some of the Germans being marched back to captivity: 'They were unshaven and filthy and all looked exhausted . . . their uniforms were so covered in mud you couldn't see the colour. Most of them just sort of stared through you, like they didn't see you. I suppose it was the shelling, we'd had a lot (of shelling) ourselves and after a while it just drove you mad. I gave one a cigarette and he just held it with his hand shaking so badly I had to light it for him.'

On the right of the 47th Division XV Corps, which combined the New Zealand and the 12th Division, attacked with the aid of projectile drums filled with a primitive form of napthalene (napalm), which burnt furiously when ignited and caused panic among the defending 20th (3rd Brandenburg) Infantry. A German regimental historian wrote that: 'The enemy's use of flame-throwers [sic] was unexpected and caused serious casualties. The flames penetrated the dugouts and men were suffocated, even hardened fighters took to their heels to avoid this new and monstrous war weapon.' As Germany had pioneered the use of flame-throwers, this view seems a little one-sided. Still, the tactic had worked and the New Zealanders joined with III Corps to their left. Further along, to the east of the corps boundary, the 12th Division, which had dug in north of Guedecourt,

102

German prisoners, mostly looking reasonably cheerful and with good reason. At least for them the shelling and constant threat of death were things of the past. Compared to their comrades who had yet to endure two more years of war, they were perhaps the lucky ones (Bundesarchiv).

was just leaving its trenches when a sudden hail of long-range machine-gunfire dropped, causing severe casualties and delaying Zero Hour. Next to the 12th Division the 20th (Light) Division managed to attack successfully at Zero, the 12th Rifle Brigade and 12th Kings Royal Rifles having a hard fight to push back the 72nd (4th Thuringian) and 66th (3rd Magdeburg) Infantry. The attacks were assisted by the efficiency of RFC observers, who were able to direct the artillery batteries. But this was not to last, as the weather continued to deteriorate, making flying impossible. On the 6th, after a short conference at GHQ, General Rawlinson asked that the attack be renewed, as he believed Le Sars could be taken. He was proved correct. On the morning of Saturday 7 October, in wet, foggy conditions, there was reason for jubilation as the 23rd Division, with its single supporting tank, duly captured the village. It was to be a minor victory though, for along the rest of the front things were not working out as planned.

To the east of Le Sars and behind Eaucourt l'Abbaye rose a small hill, the Butte de Warlencourt, which provided the Germans with a natural observation platform, and it irked the commander of III Corps, Lieutenant General Sir W. Pulteney. The 47th Division was ordered to take it but was repulsed with heavy loss. A similar story unfolded on their right flank, for the 41st and 20th Divisions of XIV Corps. The 41st attempted to advance, but under observation from the Butte they were stopped by a heavy barrage of machine-gunfire that proved so damaging, the men of the 124th Brigade were forced to dig in. When they withdrew, casualties amounted to around 75 per cent of the attacking force. The 12th Division fared little better, for although they reached their objectives – the trenches just north of Guedecourt – their ranks were so thinned by gunfire, they were not strong enough to hold onto their gains. To the south-west of the village, where the line curved down to Lesboeufs, the XIV Corps was having mixed fortunes in taking the German third line. The 20th Division's 12th Kings Own and 7th King's Regiment stormed the German trenches, which were fragmented and not properly connected. To their right a mixed force, comprising 6th Ox & Bucks Light Infantry and 12th Rifle Brigade, overran these defences and dug in. Meanwhile, the 56th Division, attacking around the northernmost edges of Lesboeufs, was not so fortunate: although some gains were made – by the 1/14th London Scottish – they were insufficient to secure the line. The situation was not helped by the French to their right, who, instead of advancing north had mistakenly turned east.

During the October nights the Germans had been industrious, erecting fresh wire defences, deepening their trenches, and placing machine-gun posts. Attacking forces often found that ground devoid of any sign of defence the previous day was strongly protected the following morning. This was certainly the case for the Canadians of the 1st and 3rd Divisions, who tried to advance beyond Le Sars. On the extreme left flank they encountered wire in the grass, and some battalions, such as the 49th Edmonton, took heavy casualties as they tried to advance. The same story was true for the 1st Division to their right, whose 13th Royal Highlanders encountered the same problem. Elsewhere, the attack was generally a failure. Neither III nor XIV Corps were able to move forward, although small elements of 70th Brigade to the north-west of Le Sars managed to enter and hold trenches close to the formidable Quadrilateral. For the next few days reinforcements and tidying up took place, and a renewed effort was made in the early afternoon of the 12th by infantry attached to III, XV and XIV Corps. The III Corps took a minimal 200 yards (182.8m) of ground around Le Sars for the loss of over 1,000 men, while the 30th and 12th Divisions to the right lost heavily from enemy fire and uncut wire, which forced the infantry to take cover in shell holes and return after dark. Wisely perhaps, in view of these failures, no attacks were launched on Friday the 13th, and only some limited movement was made by XIV Corps the following day. The weather continued to deteriorate, with heavy rain most days, making mud that sapped strength, any physical work requiring the utmost stamina. Private G. Wells of the RAMC was a stretcher-bearer and he recounted a dilemma regularly faced:

'We usually went out and collected anyone who was alive, it didn't matter how badly wounded they were, but as the ground got worse we didn't have the strength to bring them all in. It took eight men in relays to carry one stretcher and sometimes we had to give up because we just didn't have the strength to keep holding them. We often sank to our knees in the mud and so we had to decide who was worth the effort . . . the very badly wounded ones got left behind. We'd give them morphine and say we'd come back but we had to harden ourselves to it. It was the only way, we couldn't save them all.'

On 18 October more attacks were made along the front from Le Sars to Lesboeufs. The III Corps was using the South Africans, among other units, in the 9th Division around the Butte de Warlencourt, and the Springboks managed to take the German trenches, while the 26th Brigade pushed on to the trenches running to the east. To their right the 30th Division (XV Corps), supported by two tanks, was to advance against experienced Bavarian troops, who held a line running roughly east to west behind Eaucourt l'Abbaye. Unfortunately, one tank became mired in the mud and the other broke down, though it redeemed itself by restarting and terrorizing a section of German

A German 77mm field gun, quick-firing and accurate. As the shell arrived so swiftly the sound of its flight and the resultant explosion were almost simultaneous, resulting in the nickname 'whizz-bang'. Such guns were regarded as high priority targets by British artillery (Bundesarchiv).

trench for half an hour. Alas, the accompanying troops were so tired they could not take the trench and the tank was forced to retire. The 12th Division had problems too: in part because their left flank was exposed to German machine-gunfire from beyond Guedecourt. They did manage to reach enemy lines, but were too few to fend off determined counter-attacks, and were forced to retire by late afternoon. The 4th and 6th Divisions working under the command of XIV Corps were fresh and had not yet been worn down by the conditions, but it was only the 6th who managed to make any gains, the 14th Durham Light Infantry getting into the trenches behind Guedecourt and eventually contacting elements of the West Yorkshire Regiment on their right. The 4th Division made little ground, and apart from contacting the French to their right, achieved little. The front remained fairly static for the next few days,

1–31 October: The Battle of Transloy Ridge

with small bombing parties attempting to force reluctant Germans from dugouts and trenches.

It was not until 23 October that any activity began on XIV Corps' front, when an attack by the 8th and 4th Divisions was scheduled for 2.30pm. They were to advance with artillery support on a line between Guedecourt and Lesboeufs, with the aim of breaking through the German lines and taking Le Transloy, which lay a little over 2,000 yards (1.8km) beyond and between the two villages. The enemy infantry holding the line – the 19th (1st Posen) Infantry and the 2nd Pomeranian Grenadiers – were mostly hardened veterans, and as the 23rd and 24th Brigades moved forward they were met with heavy, accurate fire. The 24th did manage some success, pushing the Germans from the trenches east of Guedecourt and engaging in a spirited bombing battle to keep control, but on their right there was mixed fortunes for the 25th Brigade. Some men of the 2nd Scottish Rifles got into the front-line trenches but were pushed out. The men of the 2nd Lincolnshire Regiment did not even get that far, being met with such sustained rifle and machine-gunfire they were forced back, having lost some 50 per cent of their force. On their right the 4th Division were attacking behind Lesboeufs, but they too suffered from heavy machine-gunfire and so little progress was made. It was a depressingly similar story for the Canadian Corps, which had moved up to relieve the troops around Le Sars, but when, on the 25th, they tried to eject the Germans from the heavily defended trenches behind it, they met stiff resistance and had to retire, suffering many casualties.

As the army gradually became bogged down in the mud the movement of troops began to slow as roads became impassable and duckboard tracks floated away. It was left to XIV Corps' 33rd Division to carry out the last significant action for October, when, over the weekend of the 28th and 29th, they tried in vain to assault the stout Pomeranian defenders dug in beyond Lesboeufs. But with the ground now a stinking swamp, over which movement was almost impossible, the action inevitably failed. Private Wells, RAMC recalled that after the attack, wounded men streamed back to his Aid Post: 'They were quite done in despite abandoning all their equipment they were barely able to stand upright. One chap with a bullet wound in his shoulder told me it had taken him six hours to move 250 yards [228.6m]. A lot of the wounded in the line just died where they were, no one could get to them.' So terrible were the conditions (worse in fact than the Passchendaele battles of the following year) the Australian Official History termed them 'the worst ever known'. As the British advance slowed to a

The Somme Mud

The Somme mud was infamous for its adhesive qualities and weight, being largely chalk-based mixed with elements of clay. The reason for the rapid transition from dry ground to quagmire was the incessant shelling. As shells repeatedly blew the soil into the air, it took on a powder-like form which created thick, choking dust in the heat, but once wet, turned almost instantly into the consistency of porridge. Weighed down with equipment men could simply be swallowed up in the huge shell craters, and this is one of the reasons for the vast number of soldiers (73,000) who have no known grave and are commemorated on the Thiepval Memorial.

crawl, the Germans quietly continued to slip back to their new, fortified position, the Hindenberg Line. Private G. Ellis of the 1st Middlesex recalled: 'Sometimes it felt like you were carrying half the Somme on your boots and it made everything bloody hard work. It was a white-yellow mud that dried like clay and it took hours to scrape it off everything when we were out of the line. If it got into your rifle, it clogged it up something terrible—there was no way you could clean it in the line.'

13–19 November: The Battle for the Ancre Valley

Haig and Joffre were still at loggerheads over the matter of the Somme offensive and Joffre was uncomfortable about what he perceived to be a continued lack of determination on the part of the British to pursue the offensive to its logical conclusion. Neither he nor Haig were oblivious to the tactical situation on the southern sector and the limitations the weather had placed on the movement of men and supplies. But Foch was keen the attack be continued and the pressure maintained on the Germans, who he felt would soon buckle under the strain. It was General Gough who came up with a plan that the offensive be renewed not in the south, but in the northern sector along the Ancre, from Serre, Beaumont Hamel to Grandcourt. While Haig was not enthusiastic, it was clear there was little chance of a breakthrough in the south. There had not been much activity in the north since the ill-fated attacks of July, and any fighting there would involve divisions that had not been worn-out by the heavy demands further along the front. More importantly, it was hoped the ground was still reasonably firm underfoot, which would enable both troops and tanks to be used to their best effect. The plan was to attack

13–19 November: The Battle for the Ancre Valley

over a reasonably compact front, with XIII Corps in the north between Hebertune and Serre, tasked with protecting the flank of V Corps. Their area of attack was a line running southwards and slightly east, between Serre to Beaucourt, on the edge of the River Ancre. South of the Ancre, between the Schwaben Redoubt and St Pierre Divion, II Corps was to push back any remaining Germans from their trenches and advance towards Grandcourt. This would hopefully secure all the old objectives of 1 July, while enabling the troops to advance some 1,000 yards (914.4m) further forward, taking Serre and the ridge behind Beaumont Hamel, as well as the village of Beaucourt. The original plan, which called for the attack to be launched at the end of October, was postponed until 13 November because of the weather. There was to be significant artillery support, with some 282 heavy guns. Another powerful mine of 30,000 lb (13.6 tonnes) was to be blown under the Hawthorn Ridge just in front of Beaumont Hamel.

Surprisingly, the opening moves of the battle were not to take place in the planned sector but at its southern extreme, where, between 1–4 November, XV Corps had attacked with the French, to try to break German lines that were effectively strangling any movement. In the worsening conditions, they tried hard to comply with their orders, but in the mud it was proving almost impossible to achieve anything. A regimental officer of the 7th Lincolnshires wrote that:

> 'Our orders to move up were hampered by the terrible conditions. We stopped constantly to help pull men from the mud, no amount of urging would get them (the infantry) to abandon a comrade who was stuck fast. As a result we were late and few in number by the time we reached our jumping off point and the men were completely exhausted. This before we even started to advance.'

In four days of fighting the divisions under XV Corps made no appreciable headway and lost in excess of 3,000 men, many to sheer exhaustion. On their flank the 1st ANZAC Division attempted to take Guedecourt, but were forced back by the defenders. This unproductive mud-slogging continued until 8 November, when even GHQ was forced to accept conditions had reached a point beyond which not even physical strength and sheer will-power could overcome them. The corps historian merely notes dryly that between 8–10 November: 'the conditions prevented any movement.' On the Ancre, troops had been moving up for the forthcoming attack and in a carefully prepared series of set piece bombardments the German lines had been remorselessly pounded by the Royal Artillery. Gunner J.N. Gull of the 22nd Divisional Artillery was one of hundreds who serviced the guns: 'We had orders to fire at set times in the early morning and then again in the afternoon, regular as clockwork. We were told it was to get the Jerries used to our shelling so that when the push came, we'd stick to our routine as usual but the infantry would go over the top under cover of our guns and they'd [the Germans] get caught out.' It was a simple ruse that was to pay dividends. Monday, 13 November, saw the attack

The Battle of the Ancre, 13-19 November.

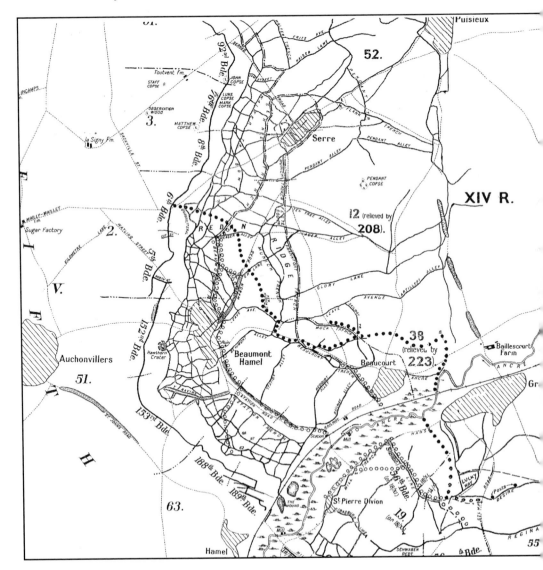

open with 31st Division attacking north of Serre along a short frontage of some 600 yards (548.6m) to secure the flank of the Fifth Army.

Infantry tactics had been modified from the traditional advance of lines of men to a far more practical movement in sections, which moved forward in short rushes. The infantrymen were ably assisted by teams of Lewis gunners and snipers, whose primary job was to deal with enemy machine-guns. However, one enemy they couldn't overcome was the weather and the glutinous mud. Although the attacking brigades managed to penetrate the German front line by 6am, they found they had a hard fight on their hands. On their flank the 3rd Division's 8th Brigade, with the 76th Brigade to their left, attacked Serre. Despite the success of the artillery and the use of twelve companies of Vickers guns in support, the men were defeated by the ground conditions, which had become a vast sucking swamp. Needless to say, attacking infantry, laden with grenades and ammunition, simply sank. Some battalions, such as the 2nd Suffolk Regiment, lost so many men in trying to advance there was no point in attempting to reach the German trenches, as the few survivors were too exhausted to fight. By late afternoon all operations were cancelled and parties were sent into the gloom to help rescue survivors.

Further south, opposite Beaumont Hamel, the 2nd and 51st Divisions were

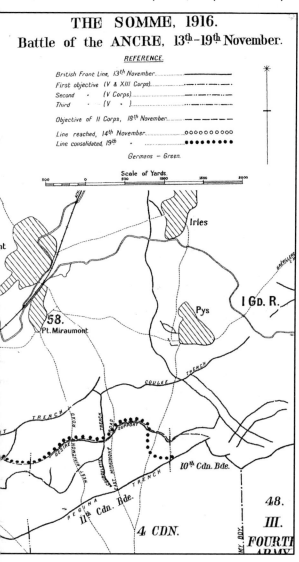

THE SOMME, 1916.

Battle of the ANCRE, 13th–19th November.

REFERENCE.

British Front Line, 13th November
First objective (V & XIII Corps)
Second   " (V Corps)
Third   " (V ")
Objective of II Corps, 18th November
Line reached, 14th November
Line consolidated, 19th "
Germans – Green.

Scale of Yards.

Snatching forty winks, a soldier has dumped his kit and makes a nest of fired shell cases and their wicker carrying containers. The cold weather at the end of the campaign is evident from the sheepskin jacket he wears underneath his British warm greatcoat (Author's collection).

under no illusions about the difficulty of the task ahead of them. Like Thiepval, Beaumont Hamel had been turned into a warren of reinforced strongpoints, overlooked by the Quadrilateral Redoubt, which had defied all attempts to take it. The 2nd Division attacked at first light, with 5th Brigade on the right and the 6th on the left. They were helped by an effective creeping barrage, and 5th Brigades' battalions took their first few objectives. But they were stopped by the machine-guns and uncut wire of the Quadrilateral in a scenario chillingly reminiscent of 1 July. The attack began to lose momentum as troops turned to avoid the redoubt and by 7.30am the reserve, 99th Brigade, moved forward to reinforce the trenches already captured. Meanwhile, the 51st (Highland) Division, had moved into No Man's Land in advance of the Hawthorn mine being blown, which occurred successfully, and the 1/7 Gordon Highlanders passed through the remains of the German line to the deep ravine behind it, known as 'Y' Ravine. Sergeant W. Stevenson DCM MM, 6th Argyll and Sutherland Highlanders wrote later:

'We got right into the German trenches – and there was nobody there! They were all still in their dugouts, because we shelled . . . every morning and night . . . and they just thought it was the usual thing and never even bothered to get out of their shelters. They never thought we'd attack in this weather. Then we went up to the top of this hill and "Y" Ravine was right in front of us. They had machine-gun emplacements and they had concrete emplacements and (the) tunnel was all linked up to them. No wonder our boys couldn't get into the front-line trenches in July!'

The attack also used the Royal Marines of the 63rd Division, who were under the command of V Corps. Apart from the appalling weather they also had to contend with the difficulties of slogging up the river valley next to the Ancre, to the Beaumont Hamel spur, which jutted out in the form of a small salient. It was heavily defended and wired and they soon ran into problems as the divisional historian commented:

'It [the bombardment] doesn't destroy the wire, it builds it into a bloody heap with gaps in it here and there where the enemy's . . . got their machine-guns trained. . . . But we got through it – some of us anyhow. We pressed forward and entered his second line . . . and there was terrible fire coming from this redoubt. It was a square of trenches lined with men manning machine-guns – and it wasn't even touched by the artillery. It was [Colonel] Fryberg who got us together and led us on.'

Having established a foothold, the reserves – in the form of 190th Brigade – were ordered to advance, which they did at 7.40am. In view of the sort of fighting that was expected, all the men carried extra supplies of Mills grenades. Furious bombing battles erupted, with the fighting ebbing and flowing around the maze of trenches, but by 9.30pm the division had managed to make contact across the river with the left flank of II Corps Across the river, II Corps had attacked with two divisions, the 19th and the 39th. The attacking force had been split into small parties to better deal with the warren of dugouts and tunnels in the German lines, one force advancing as fast as possible, while the other dealt with the Germans in close-quarter fighting. The attack in this region was hampered by thick fog, which caused problems for officers who were unable to recognize landmarks, and many units became mixed up.

South of St Pierre Divion, the 117th and 116th Brigades attacked in full view of the Schwaben Redoubt, but there was to be assistance from three tanks, as the ground was deemed firm enough for them to operate. This, however, was not the case: one tank bogging down before it reached the lines, a second breaking down and being left behind, while the third, No. 544, commanded by Lieutenant H.W. Hitchcock, reached the enemy lines, but its tracks were unable to grip in the mud and the machine slithered to a halt. The driver, Lance

13–19 November: The Battle for the Ancre Valley

A Royal Fusilier with two of the most sought-after war trophies: a Württemberg Pickelhaube *and a Luger pistol. Even late into the war, German soldiers wore* Pickelhaubes *when out of the line and they remained one of the most coveted souvenirs (R. Dunning).*

Artillery Improvements

As the war progressed, the traditional use of artillery merely for providing long-range bombardment had been much refined. Before an advance, lightning barrages would pound the enemy lines then stop abruptly, starting again after a few minutes to catch infantry and machine-gunners as they struggled to get into defensive positions on the parapets. The creeping barrage, with troops following closely behind was to prove hugely successful when properly timed. A new light trench mortar, the Stokes, was also being widely employed by the British. A single gun was capable of firing one bomb every five seconds and crews boasted of being able to have ten bombs in the air before the first one landed. It was simple, portable, and accurate, and became widely used in the latter half of the war.

Corporal Bevan, managed to reverse out of the mire and continued forward — straight onto a dugout that collapsed under the tank's weight. It fell into the dugout at a canted angle, leaving only two guns free to fire. Immediately surrounded by Germans, the tank was subjected to a point-blank hail of bullets and grenades, badly wounding Hitchcock in the head. Dazed, the lieutenant ordered the tank abandoned. Scrambling out, followed by a comrade, both men were instantly killed. Meanwhile, despite their predicament, the remaining crew locked themselves in, fighting back with machine-guns and revolvers (fired through the gun ports) for two hours, until rescued by the 4/5th Black Watch.

Meanwhile, the 16th Sherwood Foresters had advanced, much to the surprise of the enemy, and managed to occupy positions on the perimeter of the Schwaben Redoubt, while along the line other battalions were meeting with some success in occupying enemy trenches and consolidating their positions. In particular, the 1/1st Cheshire Regiment distinguished itself by taking St Pierre Divion. By 8.30am all the objectives had been taken. To the right of the line the 19th Division was aided (for once) by the weather: for its infantry advanced in thick fog and took the Germans by surprise. By 8am they had established a line across the Grandcourt road, where they were reinforced.

At 6.20am on 14 November, across V Corps' front, the 2nd Division attacked the heavily defended trenches north of Beaumont Hamel. The first line trenches, known as 'Munich', and second line, called 'Frankfort', were the objective of the 99th Brigade. As the infantrymen advanced, they suffered casualties from their own artillery, and then ran into hostile machine-gun fire. Yet they managed to reach the German front-line trenches. There was considerable fighting once they entered them and some German units, in particular the 12th Infantry (2nd Brandenburg Grenadiers) fought tooth and nail. And yet some German units surrendered without a fight. The 1st Royal Berkshires, with elements of the 1st Kings Royal Rifle Corps, pushed through to the second line but were repulsed. When the attack was renewed in the afternoon, the battalions involved came under accurate artillery fire and were forced to retire. Meanwhile, the 51st (Highland) Division, which was supposed to have attacked simultaneously, did not receive the order in time. When the division eventually did advance, it walked straight into the British barrage and was forced to retire.

In Beaumont Hamel itself, the 63rd Naval Division attacked at 6.20am, with the assistance of two tanks that were sent to help destroy machine-gun posts. Both became bogged in mud, but one managed to train its 6-pounder gun onto the German strongpoint. The officer in the tank thought he was suffering blurred vision when the ground in front of him started to shimmer white. His report stated:

'It was seen that the German garrison, some 400 in number, appeared to have found something white to wave in a token of surrender. The situation was rather an embarrassing one for so small a number as the crews of two tanks to deal with. Fortunately however, with the assistance of the infantry it was possible to mop-up these 400 prisoners before they realized that both the tanks were stuck and out of action.'

The 190th Brigade captured Beaucourt, as well as 500 Germans, and its troops continued their advance toward the enemy trenches beyond the village. As night fell, the 13th Battalions Kings Royal Rifles, Rifle Brigade, and Royal Fusiliers, dug in and consolidated. But enemy fire did not slacken, as Sergeant C.M. Williams MM, 13th Rifle Brigade, later remembered:

'Our left flank came under heavy sniper and machine-gunfire, because the battalion to our left hadn't got forward. I was in a shell hole with three of my machine-gunners and I shouted at the men who were round about to drop down and take cover. Three riflemen made a dash for a shell hole . . . and just as they got alongside our position, they were caught in a burst of fire and they literally fell in on top of us. All dead, all killed outright.'

Next day, the 2nd Division, working with the Highlanders, renewed their attempt to take and consolidate 'Munich' and 'Frankfort' trenches, again to be assisted by two tanks, both of which sank before they reaching their starting point. One of the major problems facing the divisional commanders was the weather, which was, by now, so bad, battalions could stand no more than forty-eight hours in the line before men began to suffer from exposure. All along the line, units were pulled back to be replaced by fresh troops. Meanwhile, fighting patrols sent out along the front found much of the hotly contested front line was now deserted. The Germans had pulled back during the night. Haig had declared himself happy with progress, but General Gough argued forcefully that one more effort could secure Grandcourt and Haig agreed ...

Aftermath

O n Saturday 18 November the rain turned to snow, covering tracks, obscuring the white guide tapes laid down to assist the infantry and tanks to their objectives, and freezing over waterlogged shell holes. Thus, any kind of movement was made perilous in the extreme. And yet V Corps attempted to attack once more, along the west end of the 'Munich' and 'Frankfort' lines, but was hampered by machine-gunfire and a biting wind, driving sleet into the soldiers' faces. Defence was sporadic, with some battalions, such as the 16th Highland Light Infantry (The Glasgow Boys Brigade), suffering heavy casualties as they advanced. But they succeeded in entering the German lines. There they held out for a remarkable three days, until the forty-five survivors, almost all badly wounded, surrendered after running out of ammunition and water.

To their left, British troops stormed the German lines, bombing their way down the trenches, some units getting as far as Serre. The 2nd Manchesters had a gruelling time, as Private W. Wells (brother of Private G. Wells RAMC) recounted to the author:

> 'We had had a terrible time getting up to the line and the weather was freezing. We had rum at dawn but we'd got so cold I don't recall it made a jot of difference. We got across No Man's Land and into Jerry's trenches, then we had to fight our way along. It was a nightmare, snow, mud and bodies everywhere with the bombs going off and bullets cracking past. I don't remember much of it really . . . it was like a film but I do recall the awful noise, which was a constant roar. We went out as a company and came back less than a platoon.'

Simultaneously, II Corps' troops had attacked on the right of the line, from Grandcourt, south-east to the border with the French Fourth Army opposite Pys, in the extreme south-east. This involved the 19th, 18th, and the 4th

Canadian Divisions. The 19th attacked across snow-covered ground, which concealed every conceivable obstacle, including, unfortunately for them, uncut wire. Most of the 8th Staffordshire Regiment fell to the Germans' Maxim guns in and around Grandcourt, but the units to their right were slightly more fortunate, and men of the 8th Gloucesters fought their way to the western edge of the village, where they commenced a running grenade battle with the defenders, eventually pushing them out. To their left, men of the 56th Brigade worked round Grandcourt to the strongpoint called Baillescourt Farm, overrunning it and contacting flank parties of V Corps. Along the line to the east, the 18th Division had used the tried and tested tactic of putting the attacking troops into No Man's Land before the advance. In this instance it paid of, initially, as infantry from the brigade took their objective within two hours, but they were let down by the failure of neighbouring units to capture trenches south of Grandcourt. This left advanced parties of the 18th Division open to enfilade fire: the 7th Queens Royal West Surreys were practically wiped out by a storm of shellfire. Some platoons of the 7th Royal West Kent Regiment did reach their objective, the second line known as Desire Trench but they had no support, and the Germans still held much of the high ground, which they made effective use of, by directing machine-gunfire onto scattered British units below. The Canadians had also moved towards the right edge of the corps line, opposite Miramont, to provide flanking cover for the corps' assault to their left. They came under sustained fire from the Pys–Miramont area, as well as

from strongpoints in the German third defence line. However, they persevered, and despite confusion caused by the snow blotting out landmarks, managed to achieve their objectives. The 11th Brigade, with the 38th, 54th, 75th and 87th Canadian Battalions, entered Desire Trench and evicted the occupants. To their right, the 50th Calgary Battalion and a company of the 46th Saskatchewan linked their line with the newly taken trench and formed a flank guard. Unfortunately, by dusk, many forward units had been forced to fall back. They dug in, having consolidated a small salient

An officer of the Machine Gun Corps take refuge in a German concrete shelter near Beaumont Hamel in late 1916. The officer's trench waders were vital by this time, as most of the land was flooded and the shelters were often a couple of feet deep in water (Author's collection).

about 2,300 yards (2.1km) long and some 750 yards (685.8m) in advance of their lines.

South of the Ancre, the 2nd ANZAC Division had moved forward against the line from Le Sars to Guedecourt on 14 November. For some unfathomable reason, during the preliminary barrage British artillery appeared to have completely missed a strongpoint called 'The Maze', which was situated almost due east of Le Sars. As the firing arc of its machine-guns covered the approaches to both Le Sars and Guedecourt, the advancing infantry was stopped in its tracks. Time and again the Australians tried to advance, even attempting to move up in the dark, but it was all to no avail. Those units that managed to reach the enemy lines found that the Germans had already withdrawn, abandoning their untenable waterlogged trenches. Eventually, the worn-out men were withdrawn, and at dawn next day almost all the attacking battalions were relieved. Gradually, all movement ceased along the front and the Somme campaign came to a cold, wet, and inconclusive end.

A Retrospective of the Campaign

Although further attacks were planned, the weather again intervened and on 19 November it unexpectedly turned milder, which heralded a rapid thaw that soon turned the entire battlefield into an impenetrable quagmire. It was beyond the abilities of man, animal or machine to cross the battlefield, as trenches collapsed wholesale and troops were forced from their meagre shelters into the open. So appalling were the ground conditions that even the British Official History — not noted for its emotive use of hyperbole — was moved to comment: 'Our vocabulary is not adapted to describe such an existence, because it is outside experience for which words are normally required.' Private W. Wells, who went on to serve in the Passchendaele battles of the following year, commented of that Somme winter:

'The conditions were impossible — no one could live in it. We couldn't get hot drinks as the ration parties couldn't get up. Most of us were soaked through and it was too wet to light fires even if we had something to cook. We heard that some men had shot themselves rather than go through anymore of it. Passchendaele was bad, but by then they [GHQ] knew how much a man could stand of those conditions. I think the Somme was worse, much worse.'

The Losses

So what had all the sacrifice achieved? In total the battle had advanced the British lines a little over 6 miles (9.6km) and in the course of the fighting some important objectives had been captured, such as Beaucourt, Beaumont Hamel,

Aftermath

Eaucourt L'Abbaye, Lesboeufs, Le Sars, St Pierre Divion, and Thiepval Ridge. But at what human cost? Obtaining accurate figures for the casualties of the campaign is easier for the Allied forces, as the gathering of statistical information was generally more organized. The number of casualties from 1 July to 19 November was officially quoted as 498,000 with an additional 20,000 estimated to have subsequently died of wounds. A particularly sobering statistic is that during the battle, British losses averaged 2,943 men a day, the equivalent of about three line battalions. For each division it was 8,026 men over the entire battle. The Commonwealth Divisional losses were proportionately greater, bearing in mind the far smaller number of troops employed: the Australians 8,960, the New Zealanders losing 8,133, and the Canadians 6,329.

German figures are harder to estimate, as they did not include in their casualty returns heavy losses sustained through shelling prior to the 1 July attack. However, all indications are that they suffered considerably both before and during the battle. The figure for losses from June–November is now thought to be probably somewhere between 460,000 and 600,000 men. This should be compared with the casualties at Verdun of some 336,000 men, which at the time the German High Command regarded as unacceptably high. This was only a part of the overall picture, however, for the total losses for Germany in 1916 was over 1 million men, as the fighting on the Eastern Front had also been raging unabated. France did not come out unscathed either, losing some 210,000 men. By any standards, this meant the rate of British, French, and German casualties on the Somme was unsustainable. Like so many men of the old Regular BEF, most of the Germans who were killed or wounded on the Somme were tough, experienced soldiers who could not be readily replaced. Ludendorff was being candid when he stated that after the Somme: 'The army had been fought to a standstill and was utterly worn out.' After the campaign there was considerable analysis in Germany about why their superior army had not comprehensively defeated the British at the outset, but the reasons were many and complex. The amateur soldiers of the new BEF proved a far tougher proposition than anyone had expected, and British tactics had improved considerably during the campaign's five months of fighting. After the Somme, Ludendorff was under no illusions about the ability of Germany to win a decisive victory on the Western Front, and he feared the constantly aggressive behaviour shown by the British High Command would simply prove beyond the ability of even the German Army to contain: 'even our troops would not be able to withstand such attacks indefinitely, especially if the enemy gave us no time for rest.'

When the weather was dry, deep shell holes provided reasonable cover for soldiers. Here a group of men cook up some food in a shell hole near Waterlot Farm after the heavy fighting of 15 July (R. Dunning).

Aftermath

Manpower

For the British, the campaign had highlighted some serious shortcomings in both tactics and planning, as well as underlining the fact that, like Germany, the country was unable to absorb the levels of casualties sustained on the Somme. To attempt to do so would not only put an unbearable strain on the country to provide sufficient men, but would also stretch the ability of industry to produce sufficient war matériel. As it was, conscription had been introduced in January 1916, and by the latter months of that year, it was becoming obvious the standard of men entering the ranks was not the same as it had been in 1915. The ceaseless demand for manpower also meant there was no longer the luxury of retaining men at home until their training was complete. Private Clarrie Jarman had enlisted on the outbreak of war in 1914 and spent almost a year and a half in England training, before embarking for France. While this was exceptional, a year for training was considered normal. By mid-1916 this had dropped to six months, and by 1917 this had further been reduced to four months. In 1918, men were being sent to the front with under three weeks training, some never even having fired their rifles. It was clearly a situation no country could support indefinitely, and embarrassing questions were being asked in Parliament about exactly what General Haig's long-term strategy was? Some suggested wryly that is was to wait until we had two men left and the Germans one, then declare a British victory.

Whether the Somme was the 'ghastly failure' that David Lloyd George had declared it to be is a moot point, for it had undoubtedly sharpened the High Command's perception of how to wage efficient warfare on a massive scale. The tactics of early 1916 were essentially the same as had been used at the start of the war and were about as effective. Sending masses of men into machine-guns, uncut wire, and shellfire was not a recipe for military success. But the lessons of the Somme meant even those most remotely situated from the fighting had seen graphic examples of how well-planned attacks could work (as evidenced by the 27 July assaults): yet these lessons were not applied wholesale: some of the more traditional commanders remaining unconvinced. So the question must be asked, by what methods could things have been improved?

Communications

If there was one area in which technology could have radically altered the course of not just of the battle, but the entire war, it was communications. The methods employed had not materially improved since the days of the Greeks. Runners were still used by commanders to carry messages to units in the field: but by 1916 the chances of them reaching their destinations unscathed were slim indeed. During the battle for High Wood, one commanding officer sent six runners simultaneously to take a vital message back to GHQ and not one arrived. Not for nothing were runners among the most frequently decorated soldiers in the field. Wireless telegraphy was employed, but relied on a network of cables that were vulnerable to shellfire and passing traffic. Wires could even be snapped unwary infantrymen moving to and fro. Thus repairs were a constant nightmare for the linesmen of the Royal Engineers. The invention of the short wave radio came too late for the war. It would revolutionize battlefield communications, enabling instant decisions to be made and passed to combat units. Until then, semaphore and signalling lamps were the most commonly used means of communicating. Not unfairly has it been said that the availability of just one pair of walkie-talkies could well have altered the course of the war.

The Tanks

There is also little doubt the properly coordinated use of tanks and infantry, over suitable ground, could have achieved major success. But hindsight, while interesting, does not alter the facts of history, and it must be appreciated that no one in 1916 – not Haig, his generals, line commanders, or even the enthusiastic officers and men of the Heavy Branch, Motor Machine Gun Corps – had any real idea of what the tanks could do in battle. It is to Haig's credit that he believed in this new technology, and was prepared to use it: though there was doubtless an element of desperation behind the decision. However, the tactical knowledge of the tank officers was minimal. Sent prematurely into battle over poor ground, with half-trained crews, it was remarkable the Heavy Branch achieved anything worthwhile at all. When tanks were used properly the results spoke for themselves, but it would be some time before they were trusted by the infantry. By 1917 annual tank production was almost 1,300, and it was the adoption of coordinated tank and infantry attacks, with proper artillery backup, which achieved success in the latter part of the war. The Battle of Messines Ridge in 1917 was a textbook example of how to plan and wage a successful campaign. There were treble the number of artillery pieces compared to the Somme, and high priority was given to silencing enemy artillery and demolishing strongpoints. In a remarkable break with tradition, attacking troops were even shown scale models of the ground over which they were to attack, and the result was the capture of the ridge with minimal casualties.

Aftermath

The Artillery

The Royal Artillery too, were to benefit from the lessons learned on the Somme. The increased use of Forward Observation Officers (FOOs) in the front line, who were in direct contact with their batteries quickly enabled corrections to be made for inaccurate shellfire, and drastically cut the number of casualties caused by 'friendly fire'. Initially, artillery units had done exactly as they were ordered, plastering German lines with shells and using ineffective shrapnel to try to clear the wire. The increased awareness of the necessity for using the correct fuzes to destroy wire was a small but significant step forward in assisting attacks. These had not only to be manufactured in vast numbers, but sent to shell factories, fitted to shells, and then shipped to the front. Needless to say, this took time to organize. Gas and smoke shells were also to become much more widely used, assisting infantry assaults of the future. The same may be said of more effective counter-battery work, aided by the watchful eyes of the Royal Flying Corps. In fact, the RFC lost 782 aircraft and 578 pilots during the Somme campaign: testimony to the high level of involvement they had in the progress of the battle. The use of the creeping barrage was effective when executed correctly, but difficult to coordinate in an era when speedy battlefield communications were virtually non-existent. This meant that precise staff work – often sadly lacking – could make the difference between success and failure. The broader tactical use of machine-guns to lay down barrage fire, would also become commonplace after 1916.

Tactics

For the infantry, the Somme was to prove that pre-war tactics had become not only outmoded but downright dangerous. By 1916 most of the old Regular Army soldiers were dead or wounded. The men who replaced them – mostly Territorials – were of a different breed: better educated, less willing to accept an order unquestioningly, and not wedded to the ethics of a pre-war army. They were mindful of the need to adapt their tactics to the situation. And by late 1916 new training manuals were being developed, which owed much to lessons learned by Allied forces on the Somme and at Verdun. Marching forward in line abreast, with rifles at the port, was a recipe for disaster and troops were trained to move in short rushes, using the far more effective 'diamond' formation. The old infantry section was deemed too clumsy and was split into four units: riflemen, grenade men, rifle bombers (using rifle propelled grenades), and Lewis gunners. These men had specific tasks to

The price of war: a dead German artilleryman outside the remains of his dugout, on the French edge of the Somme sector. Many dead lay for months before they could be buried (Jacques Moreau photo).

perform and it is from this period that the concept of the infantryman as a battlefield specialist began to emerge.

Morale

As to Kitchener's men, what impact did the Somme battles have on their strength and morale? Of those who entered the Somme campaign in July 1916, few remained to see in the new year of 1917 who had not suffered during those traumatic months. Many were simply worn-out with the fighting, the incessant mud, the monotonous diet, and the constant loss of comrades. They became fatalistic, often outwardly callous and uncaring, in an attempt to provide themselves with an emotional shield that would enable them to continue to function as soldiers. For some this façade was to last a lifetime. Most simply gritted their teeth and tried to survive as best they could. Some sixty years later, one infantryman from a Pals Regiment told the author that after the Somme, he just concentrated on one day at a time, avoiding anything that involved extra risk:

'I was going to bloody well get home, all my chums were dead or in Blighty wounded and there were only four of us originals left in the whole battalion. I'd done nearly three years, with only thirteen days leave and I felt it was the turn of those who had been sitting out the war to do their bit. I didn't care if some other poor sod copped it, if it kept me out of trouble.'

Others proved unable to withstand the stress and they resorted to self-inflicted wounds or faking sickness. Few of their friends blamed them. It was to the great credit of the amateur army that despite the casualties and the appalling fighting conditions, morale generally remained good and a grim determination to 'see the job through' pervaded all ranks. So much had been lost, the men believed the sacrifice of the dead could not go unrewarded, and they would continue to fight the Germans until they had been defeated.

For their part, the Germans were also exhausted by the fighting and their spirit of optimism and defiance began to weaken after 1916. Lieutenant Gustav Sack, who survived the Somme campaign to be killed in December 1916, wrote: 'We, the "good soldiers", fight because we are here to save our skins and want to survive at all costs. We are not fighting for an aim, not for the Fatherland, nor for a united Germany – that is all stuff and nonsense.' It is a fact the Somme battles, while they did not become the graveyard of the German Army, were to witness the start of its sickening: an unravelling of a hitherto tightly knit military machine. If Haig's battle could not be claimed as a heroic victory, neither can its critics justifiably claim it to have been an utter failure, although the price paid was unacceptably high. After the Somme, battles began to be fought on a far more professional footing.

Summary

It cannot be disputed that Haig and his generals had initially been found wanting. No one could accuse Haig of being a visionary. Perhaps if generals of the stature of Allenby or Plumer had been given an opportunity to command, things might have been different: but 'perhaps' is not a very useful word in history. Haig and his staff, like the unbloodied soldiers under their command, had learned a great deal from the campaign and this was to help the Allies defeat Germany eventually. It surprises many people to learn the level of Allied casualties sustained in the final 100 days of the war was far higher, proportionately, than during the Somme, being some 3,645 men a day. Ironically, the ground fought over was almost the same as that where the war had begun, five years and 11 million casualties earlier.

Biographical Notes

The Politicians

Asquith, Herbert (1852–1928): Prime Minister from 1908–16, he was fortunate to survive the turbulent first two years of the war. He had little interest in military matters and found it difficult to come to terms with a war economy. The failure of the 1915 coalition government and the increasing desperation with which the Somme campaign was being waged saw him replaced by Lloyd George in late 1916.

Churchill, Winston (1874–1965): Until 1915 he served as First Lord of the Admiralty and was instrumental in gaining acceptance for the new tanks. But his plan to force a passage through the Dardanelles led to a political downfall. He served as an infantry officer through 1916, but returned to government as Minister of Munitions 1917–18.

Lloyd George, David (1863–1945): Initially Minister of Munitions, a position in which he proved very successful, he became Prime Minister in December 1916. He was forthright and outspoken and frequently clashed with his generals, whom he was unable to overrule. Nevertheless, he was a solid figurehead for the country during the war years and his leadership endured until 1922.

The British Commanders

Allenby, Major General Sir Edmund (1861–1936): Commanding the Third Army during 1916–17, he proved more competent than many of his contemporaries on the Somme, despite being a steadfast and traditional cavalryman. His career was to be enhanced by his very effective handling of the Palestinian campaign in 1917–18.

French, Field Marshal Sir John (1852–1925): Essentially a Victorian general from the days of the empire, he was utterly out of his depth as commander of the BEF in the mass warfare that erupted in 1914. His grip on the situation in 1914–15 was tenuous and he was unable to grasp the strategic requirements of the war. He was replaced by Haig in 1916.

Haig, General Sir Douglas (1861–1928): Commander of the BEF 1915–18, Haig was from the traditional school of cavalry generals. More intelligent than he is given credit for, it was unfortunate for him the Somme degenerated into the stagnant campaign for which he is now remembered, rather than for his successes of 1918.

Plumer, General Sir Hubert (1857–1932): Commander of the Second Army, 1915–17. Denied the opportunity to show his abilities during the campaigning of 1916 he went on to become one of the most successful British commanders. Learning from mistakes made on the Somme, his handling of the Messines campaign of 1917 was little short of brilliant.

Rawlinson, General Sir Henry (1864–1932): Commander of the Fourth Army 1915–18, he was one of the more modern generals, with a solid grasp of the importance of effective planning and good artillery coordination. He disliked the concept of piecemeal attacks but in 1916 was overruled by Haig. Later, he materially assisted in the campaigns of 1918 that led to victory.

The French Commanders

Foch, General Ferdinand (1851–1920): He was in command of the French Army on the Somme during 1916 and was an educated, able man. He frequently clashed with Haig over the conduct of the offensive, becoming frustrated at the Allies' apparent inability to fight a concerted campaign along the front. He was to rise to become Supreme Commander of the Allied forces.

Joffre, Marshal Joseph Jacques (1852–1931): Joffre's poor performance in 1914 had lost the French Army over a third of a million men. He redeemed himself on the Marne in 1915, but was a solid and unimaginative commander, lacking the flair to cope with the demands of the Somme fighting. He was replaced by Nivelle in November 1916.

Nivelle, Colonel Robert George (1856–1924): He was the commander of the Second Army in 1916, although an artilleryman by profession. His understanding of the requirements for modern armies to have effective artillery support enabled him to achieve some success, and he was rapidly promoted to replace Joffre, a position he was quite unsuited for. His disastrous handling of the spring offensive of 1917 saw him quickly replaced.

Petain, General Philippe (1856–1951): An infantry colonel in 1914, by 1916 he had risen to the rank of army commander by sheer hard work. Lauded for his tenacious defence of Verdun, he viewed Allied strategy on the Western Front as being badly planned and poorly executed. He was eventually replaced by Foch.

Biographical Notes

The German Commanders

Wilhelm II, Kaiser (1859–1941): Both King and Commander of the German forces, he was not a strong leader or a gifted tactician. His unpopular pre-war political manoeuvring had led to the formation of the alliance between Britain, France and Russia, which was to doom Germany in the long term. As the war progressed he steadily lost control of the army to his generals and by 1918 was little more than a puppet.

Falkenhayn, General Erich von (1861–1922): Chief of the General Staff between 1914–16, his strategies were to wreak havoc on the German Army, resulting in horrendous losses at Verdun and in the Ypres sector. Despite his material superiority, he was unable to defeat the British during the first months of the Somme campaign and by August 1916 his authority had largely been usurped by Generals Hindenberg and Ludendorff.

Hindenburg, General Paul von (1847–1934): Although retired in 1914, he was re-instated to become Commander of the German General Staff for the Somme campaign, a position he was to retain unit the end of the war. Of questionable ability as a general, he was to provide a military figurehead under which other, more able generals were to flourish.

Ludendorff, General Erich von (1865–1937): Arguably the most able of the generals, he rose to become Quartermaster-General of the Army, 1916–18. It was he who was mainly responsible for the method in which the war was waged on the Western Front. He largely controlled German military strategy from 1916, but his insistence on fighting on two fronts, east and west, gave the hard pressed German Army little chance of victory.

Rupprecht, Crown Prince of Bavaria (1869–1955): The German Sixth Army was composed entirely of Bavarian troops and Rupprecht was the logical choice to command them. Unlike many of his contemporaries, he was a genuinely talented and courageous leader, and in July 1916 was promoted to Field Marshal. He appreciated from early in the war that the strategies of Ludendorff and Falkenhayn would simply grind the German Army down. Nevertheless, he continued to do his duty and commanded effectively until the end of the war. He left Germany in 1918 and did not return until 1945.

Schleiffen, General Field Marshal Alfred von (1833–1913): Although not a wartime commander, his plan of attack through Belgium and France was used as the basis for the invasion of August 1914. It was a deeply flawed plan, however, taking little account of the logistical problems involved, or of the speed of response by France and Britain.

Orders of Battle

British and Commonwealth Forces

The Allies employed forty-four divisions along the Somme front, of which thirty-four were British, five Australian, four Canadian and one New Zealand. This equated to approximately 430,000 men. The Germans had fifty divisions with about 460,000 men under arms.

Guards Division

    1st Guards Brigade
    Major General G.P.T. Fielding
    2/Grenadier Guards, 2/Coldstream Guards, 3/Coldstream Guards, 1/Irish Guards
    2nd Guards Brigade
    3/Grenadier Guards, 1/Coldstream Guards, 1/Scots Guards, 2/Irish Guards
    3rd Guards Brigade
    1/Grenadier Guards, 4/Grenadier Guards, 2/Scots Guards, 1/Welsh Guards
    Pioneers: 4/Coldstream Guards

1st Division

    Major General E.P. Strickland
    1st Brigade
    10/Glosters, 1/Black Watch, 8/Royal Berkshires, 1/Camerons
    2nd Brigade
    2/Royal Sussex, 1/Loyal North Lancashire, 1/Northamptons, 2/King's
    Royal Rifle Corps.
    3rd Brigade
    1/South Wales Borderers, 1/Glosters, 2/Welch, 2/Royal Munster Fusiliers
    Pioneers: 1/6th Welch

2nd Division

    Major General W.G. Walker
    5th Brigade
    17/Royal Fusiliers, 24/Royal Fusiliers, 2/Oxfordshire and
    Buckinghamshire Light Infantry, 2/Highland Light Infantry
    6th Brigade
    1/King's, 2/South Staffordshires, 13/Essex, 17/Middlesex
    99th Brigade
    22/Royal Fusiliers, 23/Royal Fusiliers, 1/Royal Berkshires, 1/King's Royal Rifle Corps
    Pioneers: 10/Duke of Cornwall's Light Infantry

Orders of Battle

3rd Division

Major General J.A. Haldane (Promoted to command IV Corps) then
Major General C.J. Deverell
8th Brigade
2/Royal Scots, 8/East Yorkshires, 1/Royal Scots Fusiliers, 7/King's
Shropshire Light Infantry
9th Brigade
1/Northumberland Fusiliers, 4/Royal Fusiliers, 13/King's Regiment,
12/West Yorkshires
76th Brigade
8/King's Own, 2/Suffolks, 10/Royal Welch, 1/Gordons
Pioneers: 20/King's Royal Rifle Corps

4th Division

Major General the Hon. W. Lambton
1/Royal Warwicks, 2/Seaforths, 1/Royal Irish Fusiliers, 2/Royal Dublin Fusiliers
11th Brigade
1/Somerset Light Infantry, 1/East Lancashires, 1/Hampshires, 1/Rifle Brigade
12th Brigade
1/King's Own, 2/Lancashire Fusiliers, 2/Essex, 2/Duke of Wellington's
Pioneers: 21/West Yorkshires

5th Division

Major General R.B. Stephens
13th Brigade
14/Royal Warwicks, 15/Royal Warwicks, 2/King's Own Scottish Borderers,
1/Royal West Kents
15th Brigade
16/Royal Warwicks, 1/Norfolks, 1/Bedfords, 1/Cheshires
95th Brigade
1/Devons, 12/Glosters, 1/East Surreys, 1/Duke of Cornwall's Light Infantry
Pioneers: 1/6th Argyll and Sutherlands

6th Division

Major General C. Ross
16th Brigade
1/Buff's (Royal East Kent), 8/Bedfords, 1/King's Shropshire Light Infantry
2/York and Lancaster
18th Brigade
1/West Yorkshires, 11/Essex, 2/Durham Light Infantry, 14/ Durham Light infantry
71st Brigade
9/Norfolks, 9/Suffolks, 1/Leicesters, 2/Sherwood Foresters
Pioneers: 11/Leicesters

Attack on the Somme

7th Division

> Major General H.E. Watts
> 20th Brigade
> 8/Devons, 9/Devons, 2/Borders, 2/Gordons
> 22nd Brigade
> 2/Royal Warwicks, 2/Royal Irish, 1/Royal Welch Fusiliers, 20/Manchesters
> 91st Brigade
> 2/Queen's, 1/South Staffords, 21/Manchesters, 22/Manchesters
> Pioneers: 24/Manchesters

8th Division

> Major General H. Hudson
> 23rd Brigade
> 2/Devons, 2/West Yorkshires, 2/Middlesex, 2/Scots Rifles
> 24th Brigade
> 1/Worcesters, 1/Sherwood Foresters, 2/Northamptons, 2/East Lancs
> 25th Brigade
> 2/Lincolns, 2/Royal Berkshires, 1/Royal Irish Rifles, 2/Rifle Brigade
> Pioneers: 22/Durham Light Infantry

9th (Scottish) Division

> Major General W.T. Furse
> 26th Brigade
> 8/Black Watch, 7/Seaforths, 5/Camerons, 10/Argyll and Sutherlands
> 27th Brigade
> 11/Royal Scots, 12/Royal Scots, 6/King's Own Scottish Borderers, 9/Scottish Rifles
> South African Brigade
> 1/Cape Province, 2/Natal and OFS, 3/Transvaal and Rhodesia, 4/Scottish
> Pioneers: 9/Seaforths

11th Division

> Lieutenant General Sir C. Woollcombe
> 32nd Brigade
> 9/West Yorkshires, 6/Green Howards, 8/Duke of Wellington's, 6/York and Lancaster
> 33rd Brigade
> 6/Lincolns, 6/Borders, 7/South Staffords, 9/Sherwood Foresters
> 34th Brigade
> 8/Northumberland Fusiliers, 9/Lancashires, 5/Dorsets, 11/Manchesters
> Pioneers: 6/East Yorkshires

12th Division

> Major General A.B. Scott
> 35th Brigade

7/Norfolks, 7/Suffolks, 9/Essex, 5/Royal Berkshires
36th Brigade
8/Royal Fusiliers, 9/Royal Fusiliers, 7/Royal Sussex, 11/Middlesex
37th Brigade
6/Queen's, 6/Buffs, 7/East Surreys, 6/Royal West Kents
Pioneers: 5/Northamptons

14th (Light) Division

Major General V.A. Couper
41st Brigade
7/King's Royal Rifle Corps, 8/King's Royal Rifle Corps, 7/Rifle Brigade, 8/ Rifle Brigade
42nd Brigade
5/Oxfordshire and Buckingham Light Infantry, 5/King's Shropshire Light
Infantry, 9/King's Royal Rifle Corps, 9/Rifle Brigade
43rd Brigade
6/Somerset Light Infantry, 6/Duke of Cornwall's Light Infantry, 6/King's
Own Yorkshire Light Infantry, 10/Durham Light Infantry
Pioneers: 11/King's Own

15th (Scottish) Division

Major General F.W.N. McCracken
44th Brigade
9/Black Watch, 8/Seaforths, 8th/10th Gordons, 7/Camerons
45th Brigade
13/Royal Scottish, 6th /7th Royal Scots Fusiliers, 6/Camerons, 11/Argyll
and Sutherland
46th Brigade
10/Scottish Rifle, 7th /8th King's Own Scottish Borderers, 10th /11th
Highland Light Infantry, 12/Highland Light Infantry
Pioneers: 9/Gordons

16th (Irish) Division

Major General W.B. Hickie
47th Brigade
6/Royal Irish, 6/Connaught Rangers, 7/Leinsters, 8/royal Munster Fusiliers
48th Brigade
7/Royal Irish Rifles, 1/Royal Munster Fusiliers, 8/Royal Dublin Fusiliers,
9/Royal Dublin Fusiliers
49th Brigade
7/Royal Inniskilling Fusiliers
8/Royal Inniskilling Fusiliers
7/Royal Irish Fusiliers
8/Royal Irish Fusiliers

49th Brigade
7/ Royal Inniskilling Fusiliers
8/ Royal Inniskilling Fusiliers
7/Royal Irish Fusiliers
8/royal Irish Fusiliers
Pioneers: 11/Hampshires

17th Division

Major General T.D. Pilcher (relieved) then Major General P.R. Robertson
50th Brigade
10/West Yorkshires, 7/East Yorkshires, 7/Green Howards, 6/Dorsets
51st Brigade
7/Lincolns, 7/Borders, 8/South Staffordshires, 10/Sherwood Foresters
52nd Brigade
9/Northumberland Fusiliers, 10/Lancashire Fusiliers, 9/Duke of
Wellington's, 12/Manchesters
Pioneers: 7/York and Lancaster

18th (Eastern) Division

Major General F.I. Maxse
53rd Brigade
8/Norfolks, 8/Suffolks, 10/Essex, 6/Royal Berkshires
54th Brigade
11/Royal Fusiliers, 7/Bedfords, 6/Northamptons, 12/Middlesex
55th Brigade
7/Queen's, 7/Buffs, 8/East Surreys, 7/Royal West Kents
Pioneers: 8/Royal Sussex

19th (Western) Division

Major General G.T.M. Bridges
56th Brigade
7/King's Own, 7/East Lancs, 7/South Lancs, 7/Loyal North Lancs
57th Brigade
10/Royal Warwicks, 8/Glosters, 10/Worcesters, 8/North Staffords
58th Brigade
9/Cheshires, 9/Royal Welch Fusiliers, 9/Welch, 6/Wiltshires
Pioneers: 5/South Wales Borderers

20th (Light) Division

Major General W.D. Smith
59th Brigade
10/King's Royal Rifle Corps
11/King's Royal Rifle Corps
10/Rifle Brigade, 11/Rifle Brigade

60th Brigade
6/Oxford and Bucks Light Infantry, 6/King's Shropshire Light Infantry,
12/King's Royal Rifle Corps, 12/King's Rifle Brigade
61st Brigade
7/Somerset Light Infantry
7/Duke of Cornwall's Light Infantry
7/King's Own Yorkshire Light Infantry, 12/King's
Pioneers: 11/Durham Light Infantry

21st Division

Major General D.G.M. Campbell
62nd Brigade
12/Northumberland Fusiliers, 13/ Northumberland Fusiliers, 1/Lincolns,
10/Green Howards
63rd Brigade
8/Lincolns, 8/Somerset Light Infantry, 4/Middlesex, 10/York and Lancs
64th Brigade
1/East Yorkshires, 9/King's Own Yorkshire Light Infantry, 10/King's Own
Yorkshire Light Infantry, 15/Durham Light Infantry
Pioneers: 14/Northumberland Fusiliers

23rd Division

Major General J.M. Babington
68th Brigade
10/Northumberland Fusiliers, 11/Northumberland Fusiliers, 12/Durham
Light Infantry, 13/Durham Light Infantry
69th Brigade
11/West Yorkshires, 8/Green Howards, 9/Green Howards, 10/Duke of Wellington's
70th Brigade
11/Sherwood Foresters, 8/King's Own Yorkshire Light Infantry, 8/York
and Lancaster, 9/York and Lancs
Pioneers: 9/South Staffords

24th Division

Major General J.E. Capper
17th Brigade
8/Buffs, 1/Royal Fusiliers, 12/Royal Fusiliers, 3/Rifle Brigade
72nd Brigade
8/Queen's, 9/East Surreys, 8/Royal West Kents, 1/North Staffords
73rd Brigade
9/Royal Sussex, 7/Northamptons, 13/Middlesex, 2/Leinsters
Pioneers: 12/Sherwood Foresters

25th Division

Major General E.G.T. Bainbridge
7th Brigade
10/Cheshires, 3/Worcesters, 8/Loyal North Lancs, 2/Royal Irish Rifles
74th Brigade
11/Lancashire Fusiliers, 13/Cheshires, 9/Loyal North Lancs, 2/Royal Irish Rifles
75th Brigade
11/Cheshires, 8/Borders, 2/South Lancs, 8/South Lancs
Pioneers: 6/South Wales Borderers

29th Division

Major General H. de B. de Lisle
86th Brigade
2/Royal Fusiliers, 1/Lancashire Fusiliers, 16/Middlesex, 1/Royal Dublin Fusiliers
87th Brigade
2/South Wales Borderers, 1/King's Own Scottish Borderers, 1/Royal
Inniskilling Fusiliers, 1/Borders
88th Brigade
4/Worcesters, 1/Essex, 2/Hampshires, Royal Newfoundland Regiment
Pioneers: 2/Monmouths

30th Division

Major General J.S.M. Shea
21st Brigade
18/King's, 2/Green Howards, 2/Wiltshires, 19/Manchesters
89th Brigade
17th/King's, 19/King's, 20th/King's, 2/Bedfords
90th Brigade
2/Royal Scots Fusiliers, 16/Manchesters, 17/Manchesters, 18/Manchesters
Pioneers: 11/South Lancs

31st Division

Major General R. Wanless O'Gowan
92nd Brigade
10/East Yorks, 11/East Yorks, 12/East Yorks, 13/East Yorks
93rd Brigade
15/West Yorks, 16/West Yorks, 18/West Yorks, 18/Durham Light Infantry
94th Brigade
11/East Lancs, 12/York and Lancs, 13/York and Lancs, 14/York and Lancs
Pioneers: 12/King's Own Yorkshire Light Infantry

32nd Division

Major General W.H. Rycroft
14th Brigade

19/Lancashires Fusiliers, 1/Dorsets, 2/Manchesters, 15/Highland Light Infantry
96th Brigade
16/Northumberland Fusiliers, 15/Lancashire Fusiliers, 16/Lancashire Fusiliers, 2/Royal Inniskilling Fusiliers
97th Brigade
11/Borders, 2/King's Own Yorkshire Light Infantry, 16/Highland Light Infantry, 17/Highland Light Infantry
Pioneers: 17/Northumberland Fusiliers

33rd Division

Major General H.J.S. Landon then Major General R.J. Pinney
19th Brigade
20th Royal Fusiliers, 2/Royal Welch Fusiliers, 1/Cameronians, 5/Scottish Rifles
98th Brigade
4/King's, 1/4th Suffolks, 1/Middlesex, 2/Argyll and Sutherlands
100th Brigade
1/Queen's, 2/Worcesters, 16/King's Royal Rifle Corps, 1/9th Highland Light Infantry
Pioneers: 18/Middlesex

34th Division

Major General E.C. Ingouville-Williams (killed) then Major General C.L. Nicholson
101st Brigade
15/Royal Scots, 16/Royal Scots, 10/Lincolns, 11/Suffolks
102nd (Tyneside Scottish) Brigade
20,21,22,23 Northumberland Fusiliers
103rd (Tyneside Irish) Brigade
24,25,26,27 Northumberland Fusiliers
Pioneers: 18/Northumberland Fusiliers

35th (Bantam) Division

Major General R.J. Pinney
104th Brigade
17/Lancashire Fusiliers, 18/Lancashire Fusiliers, 20/Lancashire Fusiliers, 23/Manchesters
105th Brigade
15/Cheshire, 16/Cheshire, 14/Glosters, 15/Sherwood Foresters
106th Brigade
17/Royal Scots, 17/West Yorkshires, 19/Durham Light Infantry, 18/Highland Light Infantry
Pioneers: 19/Northumberland Fusiliers

36th (Ulster) Division

Major General O.S.W. Nugent
107th Brigade
8/Royal Irish Rifles, 9/Royal Irish Rifles, 10/Royal Irish Rifles, 15/Royal Irish Rifles
108th Brigade
11/Royal Irish Rifles, 12/Royal Irish Rifles, 13/Royal Irish Rifles, 9/Royal Irish Fusiliers
109th Brigade
9/Royal Inniskilling Fusiliers, 10/Royal Inniskilling Fusiliers, 11/Royal Inniskilling Fusiliers, 14/Royal Irish Rifles
Pioneers: 16/Royal Irish Rifles

37th Division

Major General S.W. Scrase-Dickens (retired ill) then Major General H.B. Williams
110th Brigade
6, 7, 8, 9th Leicesters
111th Brigade
10/Royal Fusiliers, 13/Royal Fusiliers, 13/King's Royal Rifle Corps, 13/Rifle Brigade
112th Brigade
11/Royal Warwicks, 6/Bedfords, 8/East Lancs, 10/Loyal North Lancs
Pioneers: 9/North Staffords

38th (Welsh) Division

Major General I. Philipps (relieved) then Major General C.G. Blackadder
113th Brigade
13, 14, 15, 16th Royal Welch Fusiliers
114th Brigade
10, 13, 14, 15th Welch
115th Brigade
10/South Wales Borderers, 11/South Wales Borderers, 17/Royal Welch Fusiliers, 16/Welch
Pioneers: 19/Welch

39th Division

Major General G.J. Cuthbert
116th Brigade
11/Royal Sussex, 12/ Royal Sussex, 13/Royal Sussex, 14/Hampshires
117th Brigade
16/Sherwood Foresters, 17/Sherwood Foresters, 17/King's Royal Rifle Corps, 16/Rifle Brigade
118th Brigade
1/6th Cheshires, 1/1st Cambridge, 1/1st Herefords, 4th/5th Black Watch
Pioneers: 13/Glosters

Orders of Battle

41st Division

Major General S.T.B. Lawford
122nd Brigade
12/East Surreys, 15/Hampshires, 11/Royal West Kents, 18/King's Royal Rifle Corps
123rd Brigade
11/Queen's, 10/Royal West Kents, 23/Middlesex, 20/Durham Light Infantry
124th Brigade
10/Queen's, 26/Royal Fusiliers, 32/Royal Fusiliers, 21st/King's Royal Rifle Corps
Pioneers: 19/Middlesex

46th Division

Major General Hon E.J. Montagu-Stuart-Wortley, then Major General W. Thwaites
137th Brigade
1/5th South Staffords, 1/6thSouth Staffords, 1/5th North Staffords,
1/6th North Staffords
138th Brigade
1/4th Lincolns, 1/5th Lincolns, 1/4th Leicesters, 1/5th Leicesters
139th Brigade
1/5th Sherwood Foresters, 1/6th Sherwood Foresters, 1/7th Sherwood Foresters,
1/8th Sherwood Foresters
Pioneers: 1st Monmouths.

47th (1/2nd London) Division, T.F.

Major General Sir C. St L. Barter then Major General C.E. Gorringe
140th Brigade
1/6th Londons,(City of London) 1/7th Londons (City of London) 1/8th
Londons (Post Office Rifles) 1/15th Londons (Civil Service Rifles)
141st Brigade
1/17th Londons (Poplar and Stepney rifles), 1/18th Londons (London
Irish Rifles) 1/19th Londons
(St Pancras Rifles) 1/20th Londons (Blackheath and Woolwich Rifles)
142nd Brigade
1/21st Londons (1st Surrey rifles), 1/22nd Londons (The Queens),1/23rd
Londons , 1/24th Londons (the Queens)

48th (South Midland) Division, T.F.

Major General R. Fanshawe
143rd Brigade
1/5th Royal Warwicks, 1/6th Royal Warwicks, 1/7th Royal Warwicks,
1/8th Royal Warwicks
144th Brigade
1/4th Glosters, 1/6th Glosters, 1/7th Worcesters, 1/8th Worcesters.

145th Brigade
1/5th Glosters, 1/4th Ox and Bucks Light Infantry, 1/1st Buckinghamshires,
1/4th Royal Berkshires
Pioneers: 1/5th Sussex

49th (West Riding) Division T.F.

Major General E.M. Perceval
146th Brigade
1/5th West Yorks, 1/6th West Yorks, 1/7th West Yorks, 1/8th West Yorks,
147th Brigade
1/4th Duke of Wellington's, 1/5th Duke of Wellington's, 1/6th Duke of
Wellington's, 1/7th Duke of Wellington's.
148th Brigade
1/4th King's Own Yorkshire Light Infantry, 1/5th King's Own Yorkshire
Light Infantry, 1/4th York and Lancs, 1/5th York and Lancs,
Pioneers: 3/ Monmouth, relieved by 19th Lancashire Fusiliers.

50th (Northumbrian) Division, T.F.

Major General P.S. Wilkinson
149th Brigade
1/4th Northumberland Fusiliers, 1/5th Northumberland Fusiliers,
1/6th Northumberland Fusiliers, 1/7th Northumberland Fusiliers.
150th Brigade
1/4th East Yorks, 1/4th Green Howards, 1/5th Green Howards, 1/5th
Durham Light Infantry.
151st Brigade
1/5th Borders, 1/6th Durham Light Infantry, 1/8th Durham Light
Infantry, 1/9th Durham Light Infantry.
Pioneers: 1/7th Durham Light Infantry.

51st (Highland) Division T.F

Major General G.M. Harper
152nd Brigade
1/5th Seaforths, 1/6th Seaforths, 1/6th Gordons, 1/8th Argyll and Sutherlands
153rd Brigade
1/6th Black Watch, 1/7th Black Watch, 1/5th Gordons, 1/7th Gordons.
154th Brigade
1/9th Royal Scots, 1/4th Seaforths, 1/4th Gordons, 1/7th Argyll and Sutherlands
Pioneers: 1/8th Royal Scots.

55th (West Lancashire) Division T.F.

Major General H.S. Jedwine
164th Brigade
1/4th Kings Own, 1/8th King's, 2/5th Lancashire Fusiliers, 1/4th Loyal North Lancs
165th Brigade

1/5th King's, 1/6th King's, 1/7th King's, 1/9th King's
166th Brigade
1/5th King's Own, 1/10th Kings, 1/5th South Lancs, 1/5th North Lancs
Pioneers: 1/4th South Lancs

56th (1/1st London) Division. T.F.

Major General C.P.A. Hull
167th Brigade
1/1st Londons (Royal Fusiliers), 1/3rd Londons(Royal Fusiliers), 1/7th
Middlesex, 1/8th Middlesex
168th Brigade
1/4th Londons (Royal Fusiliers), 1/12th Londons (Rangers), 1/13th
Londons (Kensingtons)
1/14th Londons (London Scottish)
169th Brigade
1/2nd Londons (Royal Fusiliers), 1/5th Londons (London Rifle Brigade)
1/9th Londons (Queen Victoria's Rifles), 1/16th Londons (Queen's
Westminster Rifles)
Pioneers: 1/5th Cheshires

63rd (Royal Naval) Division

Major General Sir A. Paris (wounded) Major General C.D. Shute
188th Brigade
Anson Battalion, Howe Battalion, 1/Royal Marines, 2nd Royal Marines.
189th Brigade
Hood Battalion, Nelson Battalion, Hawke Battalion, Drake Battalion.
190th Brigade
1st Honourable Artillery Company, 7th Royal Fusiliers, 4th Bedfords,
10th Royal Dublin Fusiliers
Pioneers: 14th Worcesters
Commonwealth Divisions

1st Australian Division

Major General H.B. Walker
1st (New South Wales) Brigade
1st, 2nd, 3rd, 4th Battalions
2nd (Victoria) Brigade
5th, 6th, 7th, 8th Battalions
3rd Brigade
9th (Queensland) Battalion, 10th (South Australia) Battalion, 11th (West
Australia) Battalion
12th (South and West Australia, Tasmania) Battalion
Pioneers: 1st Australian Pioneer Battalion

4th Australian Division

Major General Sir H. Cox

4th Brigade

13th (New South Wales) Battalion, 14th (Victoria) Battalion, 15th (Queensland and Tasmania) Battalion

12th Brigade

45th (New South Wales) Battalion, 46th (Victoria) Battalion, 47th (Queensland and Tasmania) Battalion, 48th (South and West Australia) Battalion

13th Brigade

49th (Queensland) Battalion, 50th (South Australia) Battalion, 51st (West Australia) Battalion, 52nd (South and West Australia) Battalion

Pioneers: 4th Australian Pioneer Battalion

5th Australian Division

Major General Hon. J.W. McKay

8th Brigade

29th (Victoria) Battalion, 30th (New South Wales) Battalion, 31st (Queensland) Battalion, 32nd (South and West Australia) Battalion

14th (New South Wales) Brigade

53rd, 54th, 55th, 56th Battalions

15th (Victoria) Brigade

57th, 58th, 59th, 60th Battalions

1st Canadian Division

Major General A.W. Currie

1st Brigade

1st (Ontario) Battalion, 2nd (East Ontario) Battalion, 3rd Battalion, Toronto Regiment, 4th Battalion.

2nd Brigade

5th (Western Cavalry) Battalion, 7th (1st British Columbia) Regiment, 8th Battalion (90th Rifles)

10th Battalion

3rd Brigade

13th Battalion(Royal Highlanders), 14th Battalion (Royal Montreal Regiment) 15th Battalion (48th Highlanders) 16th Battalion (Canadian Scottish)

Pioneers: 1st Canadian Pioneer Battalion

2nd Canadian Division

Major General R.E.W. Turner

4th Brigade

18th (West Ontario) Battalion, 19th (Central Ontario) Battalion, 20th (Central Ontario) Battalion

21st (Eastern Ontario) Battalion

Orders of Battle

5th Brigade
22nd (French Canadian) Battalion, 24th Battalion (Victoria Rifles), 25th
Battalion (Nova Scotia Rifles), 26th (New Brunswick) Battalion
6th Brigade
27th (City of Winnipeg) Battalion, 28th (North West) Battalion, 29th
(Vancouver) Battalion, 31st (Alberta) Battalion
Pioneers: 2nd Canadian Pioneer Battalion

3rd Canadian Division

Major General L.J. Lipsett
7th Brigade
Princess Patricia's Canadian Light Infantry, Royal Canadian Regiment,
42nd Battalion (Royal Highlanders) 49th (Edmonton) Battalion
8th Brigade
1st Canadian Mounted Rifles, 2nd Canadian Mounted Rifles, 4th
Canadian Mounted Rifles, 5th Canadian Mounted Rifles
9th Brigade
43rd Battalion (Cameron Highlanders), 52nd (New Ontario) Battalion,
58th Battalion, 60th Battalion (Victoria Rifles)
Pioneers: 3rd Canadian Pioneer Battalion.

4th Canadian Division

Major General D. Watson
10th Brigade
44th Battalion, 46th (South Sekatchewan) Battalion, 47th (British
Columbia) Battalion, 50th
(Calgary) Battalion.
11th Brigade
54th (Kootenay) Battalion, 75th (Mississauga) Battalion, 87th Battalion
(Canadian Grenadier Guards), 102nd Battalion.
12th Brigade
38th (Ottawa) Battalion, 72nd Battalion (Seaforth Highlanders) 73rd
Battalion(Royal Highlanders) 78th Battalion (Winnipeg Grenadiers)
Pioneers: 67th Canadian Pioneer Battalion

New Zealand Division

Major General Sir A.H. Russell
1st NZ Brigade
1st Auckland, 1st Canterbury, 1st Otago, 1st Wellington Battalions
2nd NZ Brigade
2nd Auckland 2nd Canterbury, 2nd Otago, 2nd Wellington Battalions
3rd NZ Rifle Brigade
1st Battalion, NZ Rifle Brigade. 2nd Battalion, NZ Rifle Brigade. 3rd Battalion,

NZ Rifle Brigade. 4th Battalion, NZ Rifle Brigade.
Pioneers: New Zealand Pioneers Battalion

German Forces

German regiments run numerically from No 1, but each regiment is regional in a similar manner to the British system whereby the 1/1st Londons are also the 1st Kensingtons. In this list the bracketed regimental number donates the origin of each unit. Reserve Regiments do not normally fall into this category.

3rd Guards Division
> Guards Fusiliers, Lehr Regiment, Grenadier Regiment 9 (2nd Brandenberg)

4th Guard Division
> 5th Foot Guards (4th East Prussian) 5th Guard Grenadiers, 93rd Reserve Regiment

5th Division
> 8th and 12th Grenadier Regiments (1st and 2nd Brandenberg) , 52nd Regiment (6th Brandenberg)

6th Division
> 20th, 24th and 64th Regiments (3rd, 4th and 8th Brandenberg)

7th Division
> 26th, 27th and 165th Regiments (1st and 2nd Magdeburg, 5th Hanoverian)

8th Division
> 72nd, 93rd and 153rd Regiments (4th Thuringian, 1st Anhalt and 8th Thuringian)

12th Division
> 23rd, 62nd and 63rd Regiments (2nd and 3rd and 4th Upper Silesian)

16th Division
> 28th, 29th , 68th and 69th Regiments (2nd, 3rd , 6th and 7th Rhein)

24th Division
> 133rd, 139th and 179th Regiments (9th, 11th and 14th Saxon)

26th Division
> 119th Grenadier, 121st and 125th Regiments (1st, 3rd and 7th Württemberg)

27th Division
> 123rd Grenadier , 120th, 124th and 127th Regiments. (5th, 2nd, 6th and 9th Württemberg)

38th Division
> 94th, 95th and 96th Regiments (5th, 6th and 7th Thuringian)

40th Division
> 104th ,134th, 181st Regiments (5th, 10th, 15th Saxon)

52nd Division
> 66th, 161st and 170th Regiments (3rd Magdeburg, 10th Rhein and 9th Baden)

56th Division
> 35th Fusiliers, 88th and 118th Regiments (Brandenberg Fusiliers, 2nd Nassau, 4th Hesse)

58th Division

120th Reserve Regiment, 105th, 106th Regiments (6th and 7th Saxon)

111th Division

73rd Hanoverian Fusilier Regiment, 76th and 164th Regiments (2nd Hanseatic and 4th Hanoverian)

117th Division

157th Regiment, (4th Silesian) 11th and 22nd Reserve Regiments. (2nd and 1st Silesian)

183rd Division

183rd , 184th Regiments, 122nd Reserve Regiment (4th Württemberg Fusiliers)

185th Division

185th, 186th and 190th Regiments

208th Division

25th (1st Rhein) 185th Regiments, 65th Reserve Regiment (5th Rhein)

222nd Division

193rd, 397th Regiments, 64th Reserve Regiment (8th Brandenberg)

223rd Division

144th, 173rd Regiments (5th and 9th Lorraine) 29th Ersatz Regiment

1st Guards Reserve Division

1st and 2nd Guards Reserve Regiments, 64th Reserve Regiment (8th Brandenberg Infantry)

2nd Guards Reserve Division

15th, 55th, 77th and 91st Reserve Regiments (2nd, 6th Westphalian, 2nd Hanoverian, Oldenberg Infantry)

7th Reserve Division

36th, 66th and 72nd Reserve Regiments (Magedeburg Fusiliers, 3rd Magdeburg, 4th Thuringian)

12th Reserve Division

23rd, 38th and 51st Reserve Regiments (2nd Upper Silesian, Silesian Fusiliers, 4th Lower Silesian)

17th Reserve Division

162nd and 163rd Regiments (3rd Hanseatic and Schleswig-Holstein Regiments) 75th and 76th Reserve Regiments (1st and 2nd Hanseatic)

18th Reserve Division

31st, 84th, 86th Reserve Regiments (1st Thuringian, Schleswig Infantry, Schleswig-Holstein Fusiliers)

19th Reserve Division

73rd, 78th, 79th, 92nd Reserve Regiments (Hanoverian Fusiliers, East Frisian Infantry, 3rd Hanoverian Infantry, Brunswick Infantry)

23rd Reserve Division

101st Reserve Grenadier Regiment , 101st , 102nd Reserve Infantry (2nd and 3rd Saxon)

24th Reserve Division
    100th, 102nd and 133rd Reserve Regiments (1st 3rd and 9th Saxon)
26th Reserve Division
    180th Regiment, (10th Württemberg) 99th, 119th, 121st Reserve Regiments
    (2nd Upper Rhein, 1st Württemberg Grenadiers, 3rd Württemberg)
28th Reserve Division
    109th, 110th, 111th Reserve Regiments (1st Baden Grenadiers, 2nd and 3rd Baden)
45th Reserve Division
    210th, 211th and 212th Reserve Regiments
50th Reserve Division
    229th, 230th and 231st Reserve Regiments
51st Reserve Division
    233rd, 234th ,235th and 236th Reserve Regiments
52nd Reserve Division
    238th, 239th and 240th Reserve Regiments
4th Ersatz Division
    359th, 360th, 361st and 362nd Regiments
5th Ersatz Division
    73rd and 74th Landwehr Regiments, 3rd Reserve Ersatz Regiment
2nd Bavarian Division
    12th, 15th and 20th Bavarian Regiments
3rd Bavarian Division
    17th, 18th and 23rd Bavarian Regiments
4th Bavarian Division
    5th 7 9th Bavarian Regiments, 5th Bavarian Reserve Regiment
6th Bavarian Division
    6th, 10th, 11th and 13th Bavarian Regiments
10th Bavarian Division
    16th Bavarian Regiment, 6th and 8th Bavarian Reserve Regiments
6th Bavarian Reserve Division
    16th, 17th , 20th and 21st Bavarian Reserve Regiments
Bavarian Ersatz Division
    14th and 15th Bavarian Reserve Regiments, 28th Ersatz Regiment
    89th Reserve Brigade
    209th and 213th Reserve Regiments
    Marine Brigade
    1st, 2nd and 3rd Marine Regiments

Roll Call

---·◆·---

The losses sustained by the combatants have long been the subject of dispute among historians. Generally, it is now appreciated the figures given for casualties at the end of the war were inaccurate. Revised figures are now accepted as more accurate, certainly for the Allies. The situation is less clear for the Germans, whose wartime gathering of statistics was more haphazard. The figures quoted below have been rounded up to the nearest hundred, and are the best that can currently be found.

Casualties in the Somme Campaign:
Commonwealth Losses:
Britain & Ireland:	362,000
Australia:	23,000
Canada:	26,000
New Zealand:	7,400
South Africa:	3,000
Total killed and wounded:	419,000
Total missing:	95,800
British and Commonwealth total:	**514,000**

French Losses:
Killed and wounded:	204,300
Missing:	50,800
French total:	255,100

German Losses:
Killed and wounded:	Between 465,000–600,000

Proportion of Population Who Served in the Armed Forces:
British and Commonwealth:	Population 46.5 million. Served: 5.7 million
French:	Population 39.6 million. Served: 8.6 million
German:	Population: 67 million. Served: 13.4 million

Total War Casualties in France and Flanders:
British and Commonwealth:	512,000 dead, 1,528,000 wounded
France:	1,300,000 dead, 3,000,000 wounded
Germany:	1,495,000 dead, 2,580,000 wounded

The proportion of dead to wounded was around 3:1

British Losses on the First Day:*
Killed:	19,240
Wounded:	35,493
Missing:	2,152
Prisoners:	585
Total losses:	57,470

* The losses on the first day of the Somme battle were the greatest ever sustained by the British Army in a single day's fighting.

The Infantry Weapons of the Somme Campaign

For almost the entire duration of the war, the infantry on all sides used the rifles, machine guns and pistols that they had begun the war with in 1914. Most were pre-1900 designs having their origins in that great period of modernisation and re-arming that took place after the introduction of smokeless powder in 1886. With it had come the wide-spread adoption of the bolt-action, magazine fed rifle that was to be the mainstay of all European armies until well into the 20th century. All of these rifles were capable of performing well beyond the use to which they were put, the average rifle having a bullet capable of killing at 2,000 yards. The fact was that most fighting was done at relatively close ranges, and the combat that was to characterise the Great War was invariably done at 150 yards or less. The demands of mass production for warfare on a scale hitherto unknown meant that little could be done to improve the weapons which were over-engineered and very expensive. It was not until the post-war years that serious consideration was given to the type of weapons issued and the uses to which they were put.

The brief overview provided by this appendix gives a summary of the main types of infantry firearm employed by Britain and Germany that would have been in service during the Somme battles. It does not cover artillery or any other type of projectile weapons such as trench mortars, nor does it cover grenades whose development and production, while fascinating are quite literally sufficient to fill another book. Over the years the author has been fortunate enough to own or be able to shoot all of the weapons described, so the comments included on their performance are my own and reflect solely my own ability (or in many cases lack of) and experiences with that particular firearm.

Heavy machine guns
The Maschinengewehr 08.

Until the introduction of .50 calibre and 12.7mm heavy machine guns in the Second World War, the rifle calibre, belt-fed water-cooled guns developed by Hiram Maxim were the most powerful infantry weapons on the battlefield, second in killing power only to the artillery. The basis of the guns used by both Germany and Great Britain was the same design, developed by Maxim over a period of years from 1887. In 1901 the German army were the first major power to adopt the design, recognising as they did the inevitability of war and the latent power of such a weapon. The sMg.08 as it became known was manufactured in Germany under licence, the 's' standing for Schlitten or sledge, which was a cumbersome but stable mounting system devised by the Germans for the gun. The gun was a water-cooled short-recoil operated weapon in which the barrel and breechblock recoil together for approximately $^3/_4$ inch upon firing, being locked together by a toggle joint similar in function to that of the human elbow. When parallel the joint is immensely strong but as it moves back it is unlocked by a cam, which enables it to fold up. The breechblock continues to move backwards, being gradually slowed by the massive fusee spring housed in the tin cover on the left side of the receiver.

German sMg08 on its Schlitten or sledge mount. This example has the armoured barrel jacket fitted as well as the muzzle booster, 2.5 power optical sight and steam condenser hose (Imperial War Museum).

Attack on the Somme

The face of the block holds a fresh cartridge which it has already pulled from the belt and the instant the block reaches a stationary point, the spring pulls it forward again, straightening it into the locked position and slamming the new cartridge into the empty chamber of the barrel, the spent case already having been ejected. This action happens about five times per second, or 300 times per minute, although from 1915 the fitting of a coned muzzle booster became commonplace, this increasing the rate of fire to 450rpm.

The sMg08 is very stable to fire, thanks to its weight and the four-footed sledge mount and is very accurate, a trait found in all Maxim types and its reliability is legendary. Many guns were fitted with a Zeilfernrohr 12 optical sight, a 2.5 power device adopted in 1912. It had a simple, thin inverted V reticule designed so that it did not obscure the target at long range. Ammunition was normally boxed, initially in wooden then later steel, ammunition boxes each containing 250 rounds of 7.92mm cartridges in a woven cloth belt and upon firing, the coolant in the water jacket of the gun would begin to boil after 600 rounds. Once this began, the process of condensing took place, the steam generated being directed via a rubber tube attached to a port under the front of the jacket, to a water canister where it cooled and turned back to water. This in turn was poured back into the jacket and as long as there was an adequate water supply (some steam was inevitably lost to the atmosphere] then the gun could fire without overheating.

There was, of course, the inevitable problem of barrel wear and fouling and it was generally recommended that barrels were changed after 10,000 rounds, although firing in short bursts, or 'tapping' as gunners called it, would greatly extend barrel life. Barrel changing was rapid when done by an experienced crew and took around a minute and a half. The author set a new record by taking fifteen minutes the first time he attempted it, burning his fingers and managing to lose most of the water from the jacket in the process. One of the advantages of the sMg.08 over the Vickers was the ability of the barrel to be changed without having to pull the gun from its firing position back into cover to undo the threaded muzzle cone, a bonus for the crew. Maintenance in combat was minimal, being limited to barrel changes when absolutely necessary, topping up the water, and oiling the internal mechanism using the oil reservoirs and brushes that were fitted into the spade grips. In 1914 there were 12,000 sMg.08s in service, with six guns supplied to each infantry regiment, and crewed by men from that unit. A crew consisted of six men, plus an NCO and few men who faced the sound of the Maxim ever forgot it. Veterans talked of the almost hypnotic sound of the guns, which made a slow and rhythmic 'tac-tac-tac' noise, totally different to that of the Vickers. After their baptism of fire, Somme veterans learned to listen for the Doppler effect of the firing, the sound increasing in intensity as the gun muzzle reached the limit of its traverse and began to swing back to cover the ground it had just swept with fire. They would fling themselves to the ground, allowing the bullets to pass overhead, before rising and advancing at a run, advancing in short rushes instead of the suicidal extended lines they initially employed. During the Somme, these guns utterly dominated the landscape, earning themselves the soubriquet 'Queen of the Battlefield' and, like snipers, few machine gunners survived capture.

Technical specifications:
Calibre: 7.92mm
Weight of gun with 4 litres of coolant: 58 lb (26.5 kg)
Weight of mount: 70 lb (32kg)
Rate of fire: 300–450rpm
Muzzle velocity: 2950fps (895mps)

The Vickers Mk I Machine Gun

The Vickers-Maxim was adopted into British service in November 1912, in the nick of time. There had been a number of earlier pattern brass barrelled Maxim guns in use with the Regular Army around the colonies where it was generally regarded as a interesting but largely unnecessary weapon that was too heavy and cumbersome to be used in anything other than a light artillery role. However, between 1901 and 1906 a Vickers engineer, George Buckham, had worked on improving the design, his brief being to make the gun lighter, simpler and easier to produce. He made a number of significant modifications that included turning the toggle mechanism upside down, thus reducing the size of the receiver by two inches, and its weight accordingly. The heavy brass water jacket was replaced by a thinner corrugated steel one and the ejector mechanism was simplified. These improvements reduced the weight of the Vickers from a hefty 60 lb (27kg) to a svelte 32 lb (14.5kg) empty of all coolant and it became the 'Gun, Machine, Vickers .303 Mark I'. Additionally the tripod was redesigned, its over-long rear leg shortened, the traverse mechanism simplified and the mounts designed with quick-release locking pins which enabled a gun to be mounted for action by its crew in under a minute. The resultant 'Tripod, Mk IV' was to remain virtually unmodified for its entire service life although it was still no lightweight, being made of steel and brass castings and weighing

Vickers Mk 1, with its steam hose, condensing can and ammunition tin (MoD Pattern Room/Royal Armouries).

50 lb (22.5kg) and carrying one for any length of time was a bruising experience.

In 1914 the number of guns in service in the BEF was around 2,000 of which only 100 were the new Vickers, the rest being pre-Boer War Maxims. Few British commanders, the C-in-C included, could see any practical use for the guns in a war of cavalry and movement and Haig famously stated in 1915 that 'The machine gun in war is a much over-rated weapon and two per battalion is more then sufficient'. In this he was, of course, as wrong as he could have been, as subsequent debacles such as Loos proved and after some thought it was decided four guns per battalion was required from early 1915. Unlike the German army, where gunners served within their own infantry regiments, the BEF formed a new unit, the Machine Gun Corps, to crew the guns and provide independent support for line regiments. By the time of the Somme, the MGC comprised of some 4,600 Officers and 80,000 men and each infantry division

Infantry Weapons of the Somme Campaign

had three, sixteen gun MG Companies at its disposal. (By 1918 this had risen to sixty-four guns per division.)

Aside from the Vickers' inspired modifications, the guns worked on the same principle as the sMg.08 and machine gunners from either side could competently work each other's weapons if needed. The Vickers, however, had a much higher rate of fire through the use of the very efficient muzzle booster (Cone, Front Muzzle Attachment, Mk I) which enabled the guns to have a cyclic rate of 450–550rpm, although it made barrel changing more difficult. This gave the Vickers a very distinct 'rat-tat-tat-tat sound when firing, or as one veteran commented 'It sounded like a REAL machine gun.' Many gunners were capable of firing single rounds and occasionally on quiet nights, a bored Vickers machine gunner would fire 'rat-tiddy-tat-tat' to have an answering 'tac-tac' from a German gun.

Both sides adopted improved machine gun tactics as the war progressed. The German crews undoubtedly had a far greater level of experience in direct, observed fire during the Somme campaign. However, the Vickers crews firing defensively, became very expert in laying down indirect fire, placing machine gun barrages on targets at long range. By using map references it was possible drop harassing fire onto pre-determined areas preventing reinforcements or supplies from reaching their destinations. Improvements in ammunition, notably the issue of the Mk 8Z boat-tailed bullet meant that the range of the .303 was extended from 2,900 yards to 3,500 yards. Like all Maxims, the Vickers was an accurate weapon and when its tripod was firmly sandbagged in place it could be fired with almost rifle-like precision. Many years ago in an interview with the author, Private Tom Morse, MGC, recounted how he was asked by an Officer to deal with a persistent German sniper who was single-handedly holding up his company advance. He waited while the infantry drew fire from the sniper, and having determined his location with binoculars, Private Morse fired two careful shots. The Germans' helmet went spinning off into the distance. Cautious inspection showed one of the shots had struck the man square between the eyes, a feat for which Morse's gun crew, somewhat tongue in cheek, solemnly awarded him the cloth badge bearing a pair of marksman's crossed rifles.

Technical specifications:
Calibre: .303-inch
Weight of gun with 9 pints of coolant: 40 lb (18kg)
Weight of tripod: 50 lb (22.5kg)
Rate of fire: 450–550rpm
Muzzle velocity: 2450fps (745mps)

Light machine guns
The Gun, Machine, Lewis .303 Mk I

The Lewis was the brainchild of an American, Samuel McClean, who since 1910 had worked on the design for the American Arms Company of Buffalo, New York. His initial design was complex and extremely difficult to manufacture so the A.A.Co asked Colonel Isaac Lewis to improve on the design. He used McClean's gas piston mechanism as well as the turning bolt system that was similar in function to that of the Swiss Schmidt Rubin rifle. This had a bolt head that rotated as it closed, locking the breech in the manner of an artillery piece. While expensive to manufacture, it was safe, reliable and strong. Lewis added the clock-type return spring and distinctive pan magazine as well as the large air cooling barrel jacket and the company proudly demonstrated it to the U.S. Board of Ordnance. Astonishingly, despite successful trials, which included mounting it in a Wright biplane and shooting it from the air, the Board declined the gun and Lewis, faced with hidebound prejudice to new technology, took himself and his four prototype guns to Europe. In 1913 the Belgian army were sufficiently impressed to adopt the design and the British, in a rare moment of lucid forward thinking, also negotiated the rights to manufacture under licence in 1914. It was made by the Birmingham Small Arms Company and chambered for the standard .303-inch service cartridge.

Initially supplies of the new gun were limited and only three were issued per battalion but by the time of the Somme battles the Lewis had become the foremost, indeed almost the only, light machine gun to see widespread frontline service. The issue by then was of one gun per platoon, providing at a stroke as much firepower for one man as a rifle platoon. In its early months the gun was often misused tactically, being assigned to infantry platoons but used as a rifleman's weapon. Line commanders soon realised that it's high rate of fire, around 500rpm and portability gave them an edge in both offensive and defensive fighting. When advancing, the Lewis was able to lay down covering fire that ensured German machine gunners preferred not to raise their heads unnecessarily and a single well-placed Lewis could deal very effectively with local attacks. In September 1916, Private A.E. 'Nick' Lee went into action in one of the first tanks which almost inevitably quickly became bogged down. Undaunted, he and a comrade climbed onto its roof and used their Lewis guns to deal with enemy soldiers massing for a counter attack. He later recalled that with other crewmembers loading and handing up fresh drums of ammunition, 'The Lewis literally stopped the Jerries in their tracks. They tried to send bombing parties behind us but we had good vision all

A Lewis gun in the hands of two Australians of the 1st Battn, AIF. It is on an improvised anti-aircraft mount. The No 2 sits holding a fresh magazine, as a Lewis could empty its drum in under two seconds of firing (Australian War Memorial).

around and they couldn't get close. We even dealt with a heavy machine gun that they dragged up. We shot the crew down twice before they gave it up as a bad job.'

When it worked, the Lewis was a fine weapon, but technically it was a complex gun, prone to a bewildering number of stoppages – one manual lists thirty one. Its use of a clock type coil spring in a housing underneath the receiver was always a weakness and spare springs were routinely carried. Its cooling jacket was effective if the gun were fired in short bursts, as the muzzle blast displaced the air in front of the barrel and drew cool air into the jacket from behind, just in front of the forward edge of the drum. In theory this worked very well, but if the gun were fired in long bursts, there was insufficient air displacement and the barrel soon began to overheat. Unlike Maxim designs, the Lewis barrel could not be very rapidly changed and the only solution was to let the gun cool down. This was recommended as the overheating invariably caused a malfunction such as a jammed bolt or broken extractor. Probably the most recognisable part of the Lewis was its flat, forty-seven round drum magazine, which was unfortunately also its weakest link. The magazine was open to the elements underneath and when fired considerable dust is blown up around the receiver, much of which finds its way into the magazine. In addition, mud was a continual companion on the Somme and it was virtually impossible to avoid splashing liquid ooze into the drum. In addition, any sort of damage to the delicate aluminium carousel inside the drum, around which the ammunition rotated, would cause an immediate jam.

In firing a Lewis, the author soon appreciated that a reliable drum was worth its weight in gold as the weapon would fire faultlessly all day in bursts of eight to ten rounds. A bad magazine, however, could cause a stoppage without warning, sometimes after only three or four shots and this could happen a dozen times with the same magazine. This was not only frustrating but also potentially life threatening and Lewis gunners chose their magazines with great care. Private Fred Mowbray of the Kings Royal Rifles trained as a Lewis gunner and said of the gun: 'It was very heavy and I often cursed it when we were plugging through the mud up to the line. We needed a lot of drums [magazines] to keep it going as you couldn't reload them quickly so the team used handcarts to get the pans [magazines] as near to the line as possible, but having to carry those damn things was a real trial. Mind you, it was solidly made and it saved my life.' Inexperienced in warfare and doing as he was ordered, which was to advance steadily towards a German concrete machine gun post, young Fred Mowbray watched in fascination as the men to his side suddenly sank to the ground, little realising they had been caught by a traversing Maxim gun. He too was soon the recipient of half a dozen bullets one of which shattered his left wrist, another travelling up his right forearm and exiting at his elbow. The others struck the Lewis gun he was holding across his chest, the impact being such that he was literally knocked off his feet into a shell hole. It was a brief, but spectacular entry into warfare and a quick exit.

Such was the practicality of the Lewis gun in trench warfare that the Germans took the unusual step of adopting captured examples into service. Initially they were used with captured .303 ammunition, but eventually most were re-chambered for the German 7.92mm cartridge and an instruction manual in German was issued. There exists a much reproduced photograph of German troops marching up to the line on the Somme, carrying shouldered Lewis guns. It was to remain the only really effective light machine gun in service throughout the war, and many thousands were re-issued in 1940, mostly for ship defence.

Technical specifications:
Calibre: .303-inch
Weight empty: 28 lb (12.5kg)
Weight loaded: 33 lb (15kg)
Barrel length: 26 ins (670mm)
Rate of fire: 500–600rpm
Muzzle velocity: 2450fps (745mps)

The Maschinengewehr 08/15

The German army had no light machine gun in service at the start of the war, and an army officer and engineer, Frederich Von Merkatz was asked to give his attention to improving the existing heavy sMg08. It had been quickly realised that the size and weight of the '08 made it unsuitable for trench fighting, where portability and lightness were pre-requisites. The gun that Von Merkatz designed was a light version of the heavy machine gun, although light is a relative term as it weighed 43 lb (20kg) loaded. The main problem was that the Maxim design was not easy to convert to aircooling, only aircraft mounted weapons being able to utilise slipstream to ensure the barrels did not overheat, so Merkatz was forced to retain water cooling, although he reduced the jacket capacity from four to three litres. Other changes involved removing the spade grips, fitting a wooden shoulder stock and pistol grip and trigger underneath the receiver. A sturdy rifle-type rearsight was fitted in place of the fine leaf sight and a solid bipod was produced that initially clamped around the rear of the water jacket. This was later modified to fit on a spigot underneath the receiver. As the gun was supposed to be one-man portable, the 250 round belt and magazine box were clearly impractical, so a round pressed steel drum magazine, called the *Trommel*, was mounted on a special bracket clamped to the right of the breech. This held 100 rounds in a fabric belt that was specially made for the 08/15.

For tactical use, the Germans worked on the basis of a four man team, the gunner, his loader and two ammunition carriers. As with any machine gun team, all of the crew were fully trained in the use of the weapon, the troop (*Trupp*) were also given the additional protection of a seven man rifle squad and senior NCO whose job was to work with them in action. These men were also given basic machine gun training to enable them to ensure it was kept in action should the crew become casualties. Guns were issued at the rate of four per infantry company and allied to the many heavy 08s already in use, they gave the Germans an overwhelming superiority in firepower that gave rise to the British suspicion that every other German soldier had a Maxim. Certainly the volume of fire that they were able to direct on attacking troops was utterly devastating and anyone who has fired one of these weapons will understand the utter futility of sending infantry against them over open ground. Theoretically a single Mg08 was capable of wiping out a battalion in about three minutes.

In fact, the 08/15 was not designed to be used as a static gun, but was to be carried by attack troops to provide a heavy volume of fire over short periods. On the Somme, this did not always work out as planned, as gun crews frequently became isolated in the ebb and flow of the fighting and were forced to form impromptu defensive positions in which they had to remain for hours, if not days. The problem for the crews was the limited water supply that they carried for the gun, as the cooling system would eventually lose sufficient water as steam to require topping up. However, heavy water canisters did not make for easy or fast movement so while a spare water can was carried where possible, the men often had to resort to using their water bottles, leaving them in the unpleasant situation of having no drinking water for indefinite lengths of time. Occasionally desperate measures were called for, and urinating into the can to provide water was a last resort. Veteran machine gunners said this was normally only ever tried once, as the resulting smell required gas masks to be work. Despite the fact that the gun itself was almost five feet long it had to be one man portable. A heavy leather carrying sling was developed that laced through a slot in the stock and had a large leather loop that slid over the coolant jacket but it did little of disguise the fact that the gun was both heavy and unwieldy. Unlike the Lewis, it was nearly impossible for even a strong man to fire it from the shoulder but the sling design did enable it to be fired from the hip.

In combat the Mg08/15 proved to be adequate, if not outstanding. The water in the jacket was vulnerable, needing to be protected from freezing in winter and like all Maxims the mechanism needed to be kept scrupulously clean — easier on a static gun in an emplacement than with a mobile light machine gun. The bipod was narrow and too far to the rear, providing poor balance for aiming and the heavy drum magazine tended to cause an imbalance when the gun was on its bipod. Indeed, the 08/15 is a curiously

Maxim MG08/15

unstable weapon to shoot, for the internal mechanism racing to-and-fro inside the receiver sets up a fore-and-aft rocking motion that the light bipod cannot control. This is exacerbated by the water in the jacket which starts sloshing forwards and backwards in mechanical sympathy. As a result, the sights and muzzle constantly rise and drop considerably more than they do on a tripod mounted gun. This may be the reason why so many British troops commented on the fact that they were able to advance on objectives unscathed because the machine guns were unaccountably firing high. Nevertheless, it was the best the Germans had and by 1918 no less than 130,000 were manufactured by the seven companies tasked with its production.

Technical specifications:
Calibre: 7.92mm
Weight loaded: 43 lb (19.5kg)
Barrel length: 28¼ ins (718mm)
Rate of fire: 450–550 rpm
Muzzle velocity: 2925fps (892mps)

Infantry Rifles
The Short, Magazine Lee Enfield

The SMLE, was developed by the Board of Ordnance in an attempt to reduce the cost and confusion engendered by the issue of separate rifles for infantry, cavalry and corps troops, such as artillery. It was actually the first rifle of its type to be developed by any army as a compromise weapon, designed to fulfil the requirements of all the branches of the service and it must be said that in this role, it performed sterling service. It was developed from the original Lee Metford Mk 1 rifle of 1888, which followed the normal trend of being a long barrelled bolt action magazine rifle of extraordinarily fine build quality but its length necessitated the manufacture of a carbine variant and this trend continued with the issue of the improved Lee Enfield Mk 1 rifle of 1905. However in 1902, hard experience gained in the fighting in South Africa prompted the army to re-examine the rifle and the result was the SMLE, or to use its proper nomenclature, Short, Magazine Lee Enfield Rifle No 1. The Short referring to the barrel length, and not as many people think, the magazine size. The 'Bundook'* or 'Smellie' as it was affectionately known was to prove an enduring design, remaining in service in a number of variants until 1954 and seeing Britain through two world wars.

The basic design of the rifle is little different to that of most other military rifles of the period, being a magazine loading, bolt action that uses a long locking lug that ensures the bolt is inherently strong. What was unusual about the SMLE was the shortened barrel, all-enclosing woodwork and very distinctive stubby 'chin' under the muzzle that forms an integral mounting lug for the bayonet. It is worth

Two British soldiers rest in 'funk holes' their rifles propped up close at hand. The nearest rifle is an early Mk III No 1 with the long range volley sight visible on the stock just in front of the rearsight. The other rifle appears to be a later production example that for reasons of economy had the volley sight omitted (Imperial War Museum).

noting that when the rifle was introduced in 1903 it met with universal condemnation from 'experts'. Among other criticisms, it was stated it was far too short to be accurate, yet too long for cavalry use; that the sights, positioned half way down the barrel, were of no practical use for combat shooting and that it was hideously ugly. In fact, the SMLE turned out to be an excellent combat rifle as its short length in trench fighting was a positive boon, being less prone to snagging on wire or cables. The enclosing wood also gave it some protection from the often appalling elements and a magazine cut-off plate, fitted to the right side of the receiver enabled the chamber to be loaded one round at a time, although this feature was discontinued after 1916.

As a shooters rifle, it is certainly not in the Bisley class as a standard issue weapon. It is a competent rifle to shoot out to about 500 yards and a decent one is capable of two inch grouping at 200 yards, certainly good enough for a head shot. In standard form, many were fitted with telescopic sights from late 1915 onwards and issued as snipers weapons, but it does not make a particularly effective long range weapon. There are a number of reasons for this: the short barrel doesn't help but also the service barrel is too thin to provide consistent accuracy (target rifles were fitted with much heavier barrels) and the woodwork did have a detrimental effect when wet for it swelled, pressing on the barrel and affecting accuracy. While these criticisms are fair enough, in practice most combat on the Somme was at short ranges, between 50 and 150 yards, so long range accuracy was not an issue. Private Horace Smith of the London Regiment recalled that when fighting in September 1916, 'often as not we were shooting at the Bosches less than twenty yards away, their trenches were so close that if we took a wrong turn we would literally bump into them. My rifle was never at my shoulder…we held them close to our waists and fired like western cowboys as we rounded the traverses. It was difficult to miss at those ranges, it really was.' So limiting was the space in the often partly destroyed trenches, that fitting the bayonet was not deemed sensible for its propensity to snag on anything and everything made it a very dangerous friend. However, the .303-inch bullet was a powerful projectile and it was quite possible to fire one straight through two thicknesses of sandbags at 200 yards and it would penetrate a German helmet at 400 yards.

For the Regular army of 1914, shooting was a skill that they were expected to master in the same manner as any drill. They were good at it and the aimed fifteen rounds per minute that a regular soldier could fire made the BEF a formidable force to attack, as the Germans found out. Not for nothing did the Kaiser comment that the British army appeared to have equipped all of their soldiers with machine guns, for the deadly hail of rapid fire that greeted approaching German forces in 1914 and 1915 was the trademark of the army.

Alas, by 1916 most of the old regulars were dead or wounded and the new army did not have the same arms skills, although it is arguable that in the trench fighting that had evolved this did not matter so much anyway. Regardless of its shortcomings, there can be little doubt that the SMLE was the best combat rifle issued to any army during the war and its subsequent longevity is testament to its quality and inherently practical design.

> *Technical specifications:*
> Calibre: .303-inch
> Weight loaded: 8³⁄₄ lb (4kg)
> Barrel length: 25 ins (638 mm)
> Magazine capacity: 10 rounds
> Muzzle velocity: 2200fps (670mps)

* A corruption of the Hindi word for a rifle, brought to France by regular soldiers who had served in India. It had largely fallen out of use by 1916.

The Infanteriegewehr Modell 1898

Dating back to the 18th century, the German Army had a long tradition of being issued with very good quality rifles. By the end of the 19th century there was a pressing need for a rifle that was more modern in design than the old Reichs-Commission Modell 1888 rifle and under the directorship of the brilliant Paul Mauser the Mauserwerke factory redesigned the old weapon to produce the Infanteriegewehr Modell 1898, or Gew.98 as it is more commonly known. The original rather weak bolt locking system was improved by the addition of an extra locking lug, making the action virtually indestructible; indeed the Mauser action has been more widely copied than any other rifle system in the world and more military variants of the Gew.98 have been sold than any other infantry rifle apart from the AK47. The magazine is a flush fitting type, that gives the rifle a very clean look although this is somewhat countered by the curious ramp type rearsight which makes the rifle easy to distinguish from later models. The bolt handle, unlike that of the SMLE, is not curved down to sit flush with the receiver, but juts out horizontally and was the cause of much grumbling in the trenches, as it snagged on any available projections.

Whilst the Gew.98 design proved to be an excellent infantry weapon, it had some shortcomings where trench warfare was concerned, ironically one being the barrel length. This was four inches longer then the Enfield, making it more awkward to use in the confines of a trench, although it did provide better accuracy for long range shooting. Added to this was the awkwardness of the

Gew.98

bolt, which was not as quick to work as that of the Enfield plus also the smaller magazine capacity, which meant that the rifle was not as practical for trench warfare. Shooting the Mauser is little different from the SMLE, its recoil is slightly less pronounced and there is little doubt that at ranges over 400 yards it has better accuracy. It is certainly difficult to cycle the action as smoothly as the Enfield as the awkward angle of the bolt tends to make the shooter push the barrel off-target when re-loading, making target re-acquisition slightly slower and the trigger action invariably feels rough and gritty. Complaints from the infantry about the awkwardness of the rifle were taken seriously so a carbine version called the Karabiner Modell 1898k (Modell Kar98k) was gradually introduced and by 1918, it had become the standard issue infantry rifle, remaining so until the end of World War Two.

If there is one area that Mauser must be credited for in producing the Gew.98, it is something that is often overlooked, which was the simultaneous development of the 7.92mm ammunition to accompany it. The old Modell 1888 fired an 8mm round-nosed bullet, as did most other military rifles of the period. By 1905, development work by the factory had produced a far more ballistically efficient pointed or *Spitzer* bullet which, allied to an increase in charge, meant that the new 'S Patrone' cartridge was significantly more powerful than the old one. Not content with this, further experimentation by Mauser came up with a 'boat tail' bullet design. This was a taper to the rear of the bullet that smoothed the airflow, improving stability and range, although at the cost of faster barrel wear. Initially only supplied for machine gun use this style of bullet is now used almost universally for both military and commercial shooting.

Technical specifications:
Calibre: 7.92mm
Weight loaded: 9 lb (4kg)
Barrel length: 29 ins (735mm)
Magazine capacity: 5 rounds
Muzzle velocity: 2450fps (745mps)

Pistols
The Webley Revolvers

Traditionally in the British army, officers had purchased their own sidearms as the pistol was not initially considered to be an issue weapon. This attitude lingered until the official adoption of the ill-fated Enfield Mk I revolver in 1881 and by 1887 its replacement, the Webley designed Mk I service revolver, which was deemed by the Board of Ordnance to be of sufficient quality and robustness to survive in service. The issue of these pistols in .455/476 calibre then commenced and the history of the Webley revolvers is sufficiently involved to fill a separate book, indeed several have been written on the subject. Suffice to say that by 1916 most officers were carrying the Mk V or Mk VI variants* of the Webley. The Mk V was adopted into service in 1913, the Mk VI in 1915. These were chambered for the standard .455 inch cartridge although it is worth noting that even at this date, an officer could still purchase and carry any make of pistol he wanted, provided it chambered the service cartridge.

The Webley was a good combination of near indestructible robustness allied to simple design and excellent build quality. They are all top break revolvers, having a thumb latch to the left of the hammer which, when pushed forward, unlocks the whole barrel, frame and cylinder unit enabling it to swivel downwards. This makes cartridge insertion and ejection child's play and more importantly, extremely quick. Anyone who has fired a revolver knows that it is not an easily acquired skill and it is true to say that most of those carried during the war were done so by soldiers who could not have hit a barn door with one. They were, however, the ideal tool for trench fighting, as the heavy bullet will stop any man in his tracks, and at close quarters it is a very deadly weapon, as Lieutenant J. Hayward of the Royal Berkshire Regiment proved at Thiepval in late 1916. Having ejected the Germans from their trenches, his men leapt in and threw up a wire barricade to prevent counter attack and a furious bombing fight broke out. Hayward recalled: 'I used my revolver to shoot any Germans who appeared round the traverse and I certainly got a few of them. When I ran out of ammunition, I ducked into a dugout and reloaded while my sergeant took my place. I didn't carry a lot (of ammunition) in my pouch and I soon ran out, so I picked up a rifle. Then a German grenade blew up on the parados behind me and a tremendous blow in the middle of my back was the last I recalled.' Lieutenant Hayward was awarded the Military Cross for his stout defence of the barricade, a minor event he didn't consider worth mentioning to his family for nearly sixty years!

There are few practical problems with shooting the Webley pistols, although

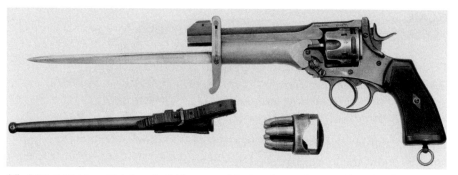

The MkVI Webley, with below, the Prideaux speed loader. Among the many ideas that the war fostered was the Pritchard Greener revolver bayonet, seen here fitted to this revolver. It was not a practical idea and fewer than 250 were probably manufactured (Royal Armouries Museum).

the earlier models with tapered 'birdshead' grips proved difficult to hold securely if hands were wet or muddy but this was remedied with the flared grips fitted to Mk VI models. The 6-inch barrelled versions are certainly accurate and capable of good grouping at 50 yards in skilled hands, three inch groups being possible with good quality ammunition. The pistols may be fired single or double action, either by using the thumb to pull back the hammer or simply by pulling the trigger each time, although the heavy recoil takes some adjusting to. By the time of the Somme campaign, the revolver was no longer the preserve of the officer, but was also carried by senior NCOs, machine gunners, Royal Engineers and other specialist troops for whom a rifle was not considered practical. The design survived almost unchanged through the Second World War, only the calibre being reduced to a barely adequate .38-inch.

Technical specifications:
Calibre: .455-inch
Weight loaded: 3 lb (1.3kg)
Barrel length: Mk V 4 ins (102mm) Mk VI 6 ins (152mm)
Cylinder capacity: 6 rounds
Combat range : 20 yds
Muzzle velocity: 650fps (195mps)

* There were of course hundreds of earlier Webley models also in use.

Reichs-Commission Revolver Modell 1879

While it lacked the glamour of the Luger, this old-fashioned revolver was manufactured in very large numbers by a wide variety of firms. It was chambered for the 10.6mm cartridge (roughly equivalent to the modern .44

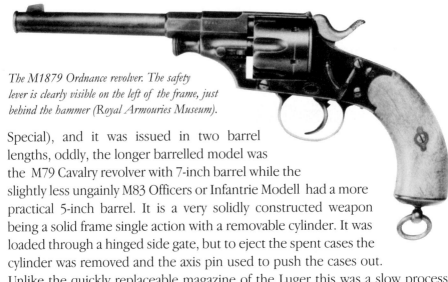

*The M1879 Ordnance revolver. The safety
lever is clearly visible on the left of the frame, just
behind the hammer (Royal Armouries Museum).*

Special), and it was issued in two barrel
lengths, oddly, the longer barrelled model was
the M79 Cavalry revolver with 7-inch barrel while the
slightly less ungainly M83 Officers or Infantrie Modell had a more
practical 5-inch barrel. It is a very solidly constructed weapon
being a solid frame single action with a removable cylinder. It was
loaded through a hinged side gate, but to eject the spent cases the
cylinder was removed and the axis pin used to push the cases out.
Unlike the quickly replaceable magazine of the Luger this was a slow process
and not something to be undertaken lightly during a trench fight. The pistol
was unusual for having a safety catch on the left side, a dubious feature on a
revolver and one that, in an emergency, could prevent a life-saving shot from
being fired. It was even by the standards of it day, a very antiquated design and
it was not surprising that from 1908 it was gradually replaced in front line
service by the Luger. That said, it was issued in far greater numbers and saw
longer service than any other German military pistol and even in the late 1930s
ammunition was still officially available for it.

Shooting one is a mild experience, as the heavy revolver soaks up the recoil
from the not overly-powerful cartridge. It has a poor grip design, that allows the
pistol to recoil more in the hand than is necessary and it would doubtless be
difficult to grip firmly with wet or cold hands. It is tolerably accurate, no better
or worse than most revolvers but its heavy, slow moving bullet, like that of the
.455-inch Webley was certainly a manstopper at close range and unlike the
Luger, it was mostly impervious to mud and dirt.

Technical specifications:
Model 1879
Calibre: 10.6mm
Weight unloaded: 3 lb (1.5kg)
Barrel length: 7 ins (180mm)
Combat range : 25yds
Cylinder capacity: 6 rounds
Muzzle velocity: 670fps (205mps)

Model 1883
Calibre: 10.6mm
Weight unloaded: 2³/₄lbs (1.5kg)
Barrel length: 5 ins (127mm)
Combat range : 25 yds
Cylinder capacity: 6 rounds
Muzzle velocity: 640fps (195mps)

The Luger P08

The Luger was based on an earlier design,
that of the Modell 1893 Borchardt, which
was a powerful 7.65 calibre semi automatic
not dissimilar to the Luger in appearance but with a
distinctive and ugly toggle spring housing jutting out of the
rear of the pistol. Disappointed by poor sales, after 1899 Hugo
Borchardt took no further interest in its development but Georg
Luger, working for the Deutsch Waffen und Munitionsfabriken
company believed it could be further refined and set about doing so.

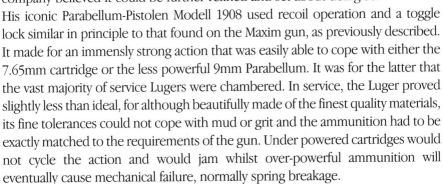

Luger P08

His iconic Parabellum-Pistolen Modell 1908 used recoil operation and a toggle
lock similar in principle to that found on the Maxim gun, as previously described.
It made for an immensely strong action that was easily able to cope with either the
7.65mm cartridge or the less powerful 9mm Parabellum. It was for the latter that
the vast majority of service Lugers were chambered. In service, the Luger proved
slightly less than ideal, for although beautifully made of the finest quality materials,
its fine tolerances could not cope with mud or grit and the ammunition had to be
exactly matched to the requirements of the gun. Under powered cartridges would
not cycle the action and would jam whilst over-powerful ammunition will
eventually cause mechanical failure, normally spring breakage.

Like the Colt .45 revolver, the Luger is a design that seems to fit any hand
almost perfectly – its grip contour making it point very naturally at its target. It
is, however, an odd pistol to shoot for the short barrel and recoil operation
result in a violent recoil that invariably pulls the muzzle upwards and to the
right, making a second aimed shot more difficult. This is not helped by a very
poor trigger design, which lacks feel and makes smooth shooting very difficult.
For very close range trench fighting this, of course, does not matter in the
slightest and many captured Lugers were carried by allied soldiers as well as by
their original German owners, but for any form of accurate shooting the Luger
is a difficult pistol to shoot, and the author has not been able to use one with

any satisfaction. There were two other service variants of the P08; the Marine Modell 1904 with a 6-inch barrel, which was in fact the first pattern of Luger to be officially adopted, and the Modell 1914 or 'Artillerie Pistole' with its 7½-inch barrel and tangent leaf rear sight. This was optimistically graduated to 800m and was invariably issued with a flat stock/holster combination which turned it into an carbine. Having owned and shot one, the author can say with conviction that 150m is about the maximum aimed range the struggling 9mm bullet can reach but notwithstanding that, this model was the one that soldiers coveted the most as war souvenirs. The Luger was the most evocative and popular souvenir of the war, thousands of them being brought home as trophies by allied soldiers. In the early 1980s the author went to interview a Somme veteran at his home in Sussex, and having been ushered indoors his jacket was taken and hung on the hallstand, next to which was a gleaming oak sideboard on which sat an Artillery Luger complete with all its accessories. Enquiring about the wisdom of leaving such an item in the hallway I was told dismissively: 'Oh, that old thing is of no interest to anyone nowadays. Besides, I keep the ammunition and firing pin hidden in the draw so it's quite safe.'

Technical specifications:
Calibre: 9mm
Weight unloaded: 2.5 lb (1kg)
Barrel length: 4 ins (102mm)
Combat range : 25 yds
Magazine capacity: 8 rounds
Muzzle velocity: 1159fps (350mps)

As an aside, many people assume the handsome 7.63mm Mauser C96 pistol (usually referred to as the 'Broomhandle') to have also been an issue sidearm during the war. Whilst many were carried by German officers and it was a coveted souvenir it was never a service arm and those that saw combat did so having been privately purchased.

Bayonets

Usually overlooked or put into that category reserved for Not Very Interesting Weapons, the bayonet was actually much used in combat during the 1914–18 war and was equally cursed and praised. The idea was nothing new, having been in existence on military rifles since the end of the seventeenth century and even the sword bayonet of the type typically found in use during the war, would have

Infantry Weapons of the Somme Campaign

Some idea of the impractical nature of the sword bayonet can be seen from this photo of British soldiers accompanying German prisoners back to La Boisselle. Although the man in the centre is clearly not tall, the rifle and bayonet are about the same height as he is and wielding one in the confines of a trench would have been difficult at the best of times (R. Dunning).

been a familiar sight to riflemen in Wellington's army. The long, slim-bladed types used during the Great War were a development of the old triangular bladed socket types which had been in use around Europe for some 150 years. These twentieth century variants differed in having a proper handle, or 'grip' that locked securely onto a machined lug at the muzzle of the rifle and a very high quality blade that was unlikely to bend or snap. In the British army in particular, bayonet drill was taken very seriously and the belief that cold steel was feared by the enemy was perfectly true. While they might accept being shot, blown up or gassed, few soldiers liked the idea of being stabbed in cold blood and regardless of their nation, most would run when faced with a determined enemy bayonet charge.

One of the reasons for the lack of interest in the bayonet as a weapon of the trenches is that post-war it was dismissed as having been of no real value in trench fighting, as available figures relating to wounds and death by various causes list the bayonet as responsible for merely .001 per cent of injuries, many of which were accidentally self-inflicted. The fact was that in trench fighting,

Souvenirs. An often published photo, but it is interesting for the amount of booty pictured in it. Men of the 10th Notts and Derbyshire Regiment pose after the attack on Fricourt. At the front, lower left can be seen a man holding a Mauser C96 pistol, next to him a man with a Modell 1898 bayonet then among a plethora of Picklehaubes are more M.98 and M98.05a bayonets, a German radio set and extreme right a German trench periscope. Standing at the extreme left is a soldier with a Luger and to his right, just behind the radio set is a man with a gas mask round his neck, Picklehaube on his head and an S84/98 knife bayonet in his hand. One cannot help but wonder how many of these souvenirs found their way home (Imperial War Museum).

where face to face combat was at its most savage, bayonets were actually used very frequently. However, one vital fact usually overlooked was that a bayonet wound was almost invariably made to the stomach or chest area, with the result it almost inevitably proved fatal. Any stomach wound is generally deadly and most chest wounds, without prompt medical attention, frequently proved so. Soldiers involved in bayonet fighting were usually in the thick of the most desperate combat and the wounded could expect no attention for many hours, if at all. Stab wounds cause heavy bleeding and most who received a bayonet thrust would have bled to death in a matter of minutes. As a result few ever had the luxury of making their way back to an aid station and surviving to become a statistic. The Australians in particular were fond of the bayonet and one observer remarked that after the capture of Pozières, groups of Diggers could be seen 'pursuing squealing Germans around the trenches like a pig hunt'.

The types of bayonet used were broadly similar, in the Commonwealth armies the twelve inch blade Pattern 1907 sword bayonet was almost universally used. Adapted from the pre-war Japanese Arisaka design, the original model had a curved steel quillon or guard, that proved enormously impractical in the trenches, and most bayonets had this removed, original examples now being scarce and valuable. The situation in the German army was far more complex with two main types being issued to front line troops, the Seitengewehr Modell 98/05a, known generally as the 'butcher blade' after the cleaver-like shape of its 14-inch (355.6mm) blade and the Modell 1898 which has a very thin, long and elegant blade of 20³/₄ inches (527mm). In addition, literally dozens of Ertsatz types of all steel construction, often using captured blades were manufactured. The reason for this was that bayonet production was not high on the list of priorities for German industry and vital materials were diverted for more pressing needs. Ersatz types were made by non-specialist firms using unskilled labour and the most basic of component parts. Whilst they were not works of art, they did the job for which they were intended.

Experience of trench warfare convinced all sides that the days of the long bayonet were numbered, for it was too difficult to wield in a confined space, became entangled in almost everything and did nothing dangerous to the human body that a six-inch blade could not accomplish. The Germans did begin to issue a short knife bayonet, the S84/98 which was initially simply a converted earlier pattern, but post-1915 they began to be newly manufactured and were gradually to replace all of the other types, although it was not until the re-arming of the Wermacht in the 1930s that this became a universally issued pattern. The British stayed with the old '07, refurbishing thousands to be issued during World War Two, before supplies of the universally derided spike bayonet for the No. 4 Enfield became available. For most soldiers, their bayonet performed a myriad of tasks, opening tins, prising open ration boxes, acting as an equipment hook, or even an impromptu candlestick but seldom the task for which it was issued. But, as one anonymous Australian commented 'By Christ, when it was needed nothing else would do.'

Glossary

Artillery: An all-encompassing term covering any large calibre, wheeled gun from the smallest mountain guns to the huge railway guns used by both the British and Germans.

Barrage: Normally used with reference to artillery, but also applicable to machine-guns. It was a heavy concentration of fire put down on a designated area to prevent troop or supply movement or to destroy specific enemy positions.

Battalion: British and German combat units that theoretically comprised of about 1,000 men. In practice due to casualties, leave and other reasons this seldom occurred. Some combat unit could consist of no more than 700 fighting men.

Bellied: When an obstacle presses upwards on the steel belly of a tank, preventing its tracks from gripping. Also referred to as 'bogged'.

Brigades: A British brigade contained four battalions of fighting troops and often a battalion of pioneers.

Cartridge: The complete round of ammunition inserted into the breech of a small arm comprising: brass case, primer, propellant and bullet.

Communication trench: A connecting trench, normally narrow and deep that links the front-line and reserve trenches.

Creeping barrage: Shellfire calculated to land just ahead of advancing troops. It has to be perfectly coordinated with troop movements to work effectively. It was perfected by the end of 1916 and became the standard method for artillery/infantry coordination during an attack.

Ditched: A term applied to a tank that has become stuck in a trench or large shell hole. Also referred to as ' bogged' 'bellied' or 'mired'.

Division: Under command of a Major General, in Britain it normally contained four brigades each with four regimental battalions. In Germany it was a smaller unit and normally contained three regiments.

Enfilade: Machine-guns were sited so they provided interlocking fields of fire to their left and right. There was no dead ground between and they created an effective killing zone, through which infantry could not pass.

Fuze: The brass or alloy nose cap of a shell that contains the ignition system. They were either set to detonate in-flight (shrapnel) or upon impact (high explosive) or delayed impact (armour piercing).

Lewis gun: The first practical lightweight machine-gun, designed by a US Army officer and adopted by the Belgian Army in 1913. Subsequently made in .303 calibre by BSA in England under licence and widely issued during the war.

Mauser: The German Army used the Gewher 98 rifle, a successful and strong Mauser design chambered for the 7.92mm cartridge. It held five cartridges in its magazine.

Glossary

Maxim gun: The water-cooled, belt fed weapon designed by Sir Hiram Maxim and used as the infantry standard medium machine-gun. Known as the MG-08 in Germany and the MkI Vickers in Great Britain. Heavy and water-cooled they were reliable but cumbersome and vulnerable to shellfire.

MG-08: The German manufactured Model 1908 Maxim, that was faithful to the original design. Chambered for 7.92 mm ammunition it fired at a rate of 450 rounds a minute.

Mills bomb: Specifically the Mills hand-grenade, but a term often incorrectly applied to any British grenade.

Parapet: The raised, forward edge of a trench, often reinforced with sandbags and wooden posts. Its height invariably required a fire-step to be built, upon which soldiers could stand to enable them to see and shoot over the parapet.

Parados: The rear edge of the trench, built up with spoil from the trench.

Sap: A narrow trench that dug in front of the parapet, usually as a listening post or machine-gun position.

Shrapnel: Artillery shells designed to explode in midair. They were filled with small lead or steel balls that spread downwards as the casing of the shell burst, dispersing the shot in the same manner as a shotgun cartridge.

Shell splinters: Often mistakenly termed 'shrapnel', they were jagged chunks of shell casing, anywhere in size between a sugar cube to over 1 foot (30cm) in length. They inflicted appalling wounds.

SMLE: Short, Magazine Lee-Enfield. The standard .303 calibre service rifle, used throughout the war by all British and Commonwealth forces. Its magazine held a useful 10 cartridges.

Sponson: The side turrets on a tank, inside which the guns were mounted.

Stick grenade: The standard German grenade, also known as a Potato Masher from its shape, which comprised a short wooden handle with steel casing on one end which contained the explosive charge.

Stokes: See Trench mortar.

Traverses: The bays in a trench that from the air made it look a little like a castle wall. A traverse limited the effects of shell blasts and they could also be blocked with barricades and defended in the event of attack.

Trench mortar: An explosive charge fired by means of a hollow tube. Early British and German examples often fired enormous shells, but the British introduction of the Stokes mortar in 1916 introduced the modern concept of light, fast firing projectile launchers.

Very light: A flare fired from a large barrelled signal pistol, named after the inventor. Widely used on both sides.

Vickers gun: The British variant of the Maxim design, it was both lighter and faster firing than the German MG-08. Chambered for standard .303 inch ammunition it fired at about 550 rounds a minute.

Bibliography

Barbusse Henri, *Le Feu*, Paris 1926

Bone, Muirhead, *The Western Front*, London 1917

Brown, Malcolm, *Tommy Goes To War*, London 1978

Carrington Charles, *A Subaltern's War*, London 1929

Carrington, Charles, *Soldier From the Wars Returning*, London 1965

Chappell, Michael, *The Somme 1916: Crucible of a British Army*, London 1995

Fletcher, David (ed.), *Tanks and Trenches*, Stroud 1994

Giles, John, *The Somme: Then and Now*, Kent 1977

Giles, John, *The Western Front: Then and Now*, Kent 1981

Hammerton, Sir John, *I Was There: Undying Memories of 1914–1918*, London 1939

Hammerton, Sir John, *Twenty Years After*, London 1938

Jünger, Ernst, *Storm of Steel*, London (reprint) 2003

Keegan, John, *The First World War*, London 1998

Lais, Otto, *Experiences of Baden Soldiers at the Front, Volume 1: Machine-guns in the Iron Cross Rregiment* (8th Baden Infantry Regiment No.169), Karlsruhe 1935

Macdonald, Lynn, *The Somme*, London 1983

Macdonald Lynn, *1914–1918: Voices and Images of the Great War*, London 1988

Manning, Frederick, *Her Privates We (The Middle Parts of Fortune)*, London 1932

Maze, Paul, *A Frenchman in Khaki*, London 1934

McCarthy, Chris, *The Somme: the Day-by-Day Account*, London 1993

Middlebrook, Martin, *The First Day of the Somme*, London 1972

Moreau, Jacques, 1914–1918: *Nous Etions Des Hommes*, Paris 2004

Michelin, Guides, *The Somme, Volume 1*, London 1921

Norman Terry, *The Hell They Called High Wood*, London 1984

Passingham, Ian, *All The Kaisers Men*, London 2003

Pegler, Martin, *The British Tommy*, Oxford 1989

Pegler, Martin, *The Tank Corps Roll of Honour*, Birmingham 1983 (reprint)

Pidgeon, Trevor, *The Tanks at Flers*, London 1995

Plowman, Max, *A Subaltern on the Somme, 1916*, London 1929

Purdom, C.D., *Everyman At War*, London 1930

Renn, Ludwig, *All Quiet On The Western Front*, London 1929

Rogerson, Sydney, *Twelve Days*, London 1935

Sasoon, Seigfreid, *Memoirs of an Infantry Officer*, London 1928

Sheffield, Gary, *The Somme*, London 2004

Van Emden, Richard, *The Trench*, London 2002

Witkop, Dr Paul, *German Students' War Letters*, Berlin and London 1929

Wyn Griffith, L., *Up to Mametz*, London 1931

Index